Ask most Christians and the
in a war. Few understand t
however, and fewer yet have been trained and equipped
not only to do battle but to also win the victory. Barbara
Yoder sets out to change this deplorable situation. As you
read *Taking On Goliath*, you will find the pieces of your
life becoming aligned in such a way that you will be able
to overcome the enemy and enter into the blessings and
prosperity that God has planned for you.

—C. PETER WAGNER
CHANCELLOR, WAGNER LEADERSHIP INSTITUTE

In her newest book, Barbara once again feels the heart-
beat of God. This time she calls us as a people to rise up
and fulfill the crucial role we have been given in the war
being waged against every believer, over the church, and
over nations. Drawing insights and encouragement from
the life of David, you will be encouraged and challenged
to live as the warrior you are destined to be.

—JANE HANSEN HOYT
PRESIDENT AND CEO, AGLOW INTERNATIONAL

In the challenging times in which we live, believers are
being confronted on a daily basis with overwhelming,
often terrifying encounters with personal, cultural, and
global Goliaths. In her book *Taking On Goliath*, Barbara
Yoder echoes the clarion call of God's Spirit to a generation of people with the heart of David who will arise
out of passivity and powerlessness to engage in spiritual
battle that will bring transformation in the earth. This
book will empower and encourage readers to release their
authority in Christ and open their eyes to God's fresh

strategies, which will create an unstoppable force for change. Warriors, arise!

—JANE HAMON
CHRISTIAN INTERNATIONAL MINISTRIES

Taking On Goliath is close to my heart. It takes a glimpse at what God has been saying to many spiritual leaders about America's cultural and societal dilemmas. Barbara Yoder, however, brings a fresh emphasis on what we can actually do to turn the tide of what seems to be an overwhelming onslaught of darkness. She amplifies the story of David and Goliath to demonstrate the struggles we face. The problems in our nation may seem like giants, and we may feel impotent to make a difference. Yet, if we implement what Barbara has shared in these pages, our families, communities, cities, and ultimately the nation will be impacted. She truly believes in the power of one. Don't be left watching the action. Read this book and become an active participant in this generation of warriors.

—HARRY R. JACKSON JR.
SENIOR PASTOR, HOPE CHRISTIAN CHURCH
FOUNDER AND PRESIDENT
HIGH IMPACT LEADERSHIP COALITION

Barbara Yoder is a leader of leaders with keen practical insight and clear spiritual discernment. Her growing international influence is helping mobilize the church into health and action. I highly recommend her latest book as a tool to fuel your zeal and sharpen your focus. Read at your own risk…this book will reshape your priorities!

—ROBERT STEARNS
FOUNDER AND EXECUTIVE DIRECTOR
EAGLES' WINGS

Written from a veteran warrior to a rising generation of warriors, this book couldn't have come at a better time. As you read *Taking On Goliath*, passion will be awakened, boldness will arise, and you will discover the spirit of the warrior Christ in you!

—Dutch Sheets
Dutch Sheets Ministries

TAKING ON
GOLIATH

TAKING ON GOLIATH

GOLIATH

BARBARA J. YODER

Charisma
HOUSE
A STRANG COMPANY

TAKING ON GOLIATH by Barbara J. Yoder
Published by Charisma House
A Strang Company
600 Rinehart Road
Lake Mary, Florida 32746
www.strangdirect.com

Scripture quotations marked THE MESSAGE are from The Message: The Bible in Contemporary English, copyright © 1993, 1994, 1995, 1996, 2000, 2001, 2002. Used by permission of NavPress Publishing Group.

Scripture quotations marked TLB are from The Living Bible. Copyright © 1971. Used by permission of Tyndale House Publishers, Inc., Wheaton, IL 60189. All rights reserved.

Scripture quotations marked YLT are from the Young's Literal Translation of the Bible.

Design Director: Bill Johnson
Cover design by Jerry Pomales

Library of Congress Cataloging-in-Publication Data
Yoder, Barbara J.
  Taking on Goliath / Barbara Yoder. -- 1st ed.
      p. cm.
  Includes bibliographical references.
  ISBN 978-1-59979-227-9
  1. Spiritual warfare. 2. David, King of Israel. 3. Goliath (Biblical giant) I. Title.
  BV4509.5.Y63 2009
  243--dc22
                        2008041842

First Edition

09 10 11 12 13 — 987654321
Printed in the United States of America

Contents

Foreword

Isaiah 53:8 asks, "Who will declare His generation?" *Taking On Goliath* is a book of declaration.

The word *generation* is linked with the concept of "revolution," or period of time. Within the pages of this book, Barbara Yoder has captured the mind-set that is necessary to create a revolution in our time. She challenges us not to agree with the norm, with structures that are contrary to God's kingdom plan, but rather to embrace the course that will cause our society to be filled with the presence of the holy God. In other words, read the principles and then declare into your ministry, territory, city, or nation what has been exampled here.

The power of decreeing or declaring will reverse and defy the time that has been robbed, as well as the decay that has passed from one season to another season.

Every generation has its own identity. Some generations live in boundary conflicts. Some have more skirmishes over supply systems and structures. Most generations, however, have to contend with ideological altercations and disagreements. As Ecclesiastes 3:8 says, there is a "time of war," and some generations are allotted that time as "their time" to live in the earth realm.

With the evident division of good and evil forming in almost every arena of life, we must be a people who learn how to discern and do battle. Not only does this book define the times we are living in, but it has also given us a practical way of expressing our identity for a season. We must be a body of people, living at the same time in this given period of history, who decree that righteousness will overcome darkness in the earth. We are a generation at war!

We must train our senses to discern good and evil. Hebrews 5:14 says, "But solid food belongs to those who are of full age, that is, those who by reason of use have their senses exercised to discern both good and evil."

We discern by the Word and the Spirit. That means the Word of God must come alive again for many of us! My greatest concern for this generation is that we lay down what we know and allow the Spirit of the Lord to teach us His strategies for victory, new and fresh.

Most of the books I have written are linked with the concept of spiritual war. We must be aware that we have an enemy that opposes us. The anti-Christ force in the earth continues to work, from generation to generation. The Spirit of God is the restraining force against this spirit. From generation to generation we must be a people who embrace His Spirit and withstand the spirit of evil that longs to increase in the earth to prevent God's fullness. We must be a warrior generation that serves as an enforcer of God's way in the earth. The primary cause behind the escalation of wars, both physical and spiritual, is this anti-Christ force. Actually, I believe there will be war in all of the foreseeable generations ahead. We must be a generation that knows the pain and glory of victory. Even in the pain of our defeats, we must always remember that through Christ, victory lies ahead. This book is one of those reminders that should be read over and over.

We are at a unique stage in our world's history. At this time, everyone in America has experienced and been part of some conflict that falls under the definition of war. If you live in another nation, you likely have a similar, war-influenced history. Remember, war is in our bloodline. After spending a couple of decades awakening from our slumber, we now have an awareness of the need for spiritual warfare. It is crucial that we all understand the real war that we are fighting.

We must be a people who not only war in this generation but also pass a warrior understanding to the next generation that is arising. One of the primary reasons God allows us to see into the future is for the benefit of the generations who are arising. We must prepare the way for God's best in the lives of those who will follow. The Lord doesn't give us glimpses just to titillate us or make us long for better days ahead. The vision of God—which we all need—always has a divine purpose.

Another reason God supplies prophetic vision is for strategy. This allows us to have foresight to develop plans so that when we face our enemies we are not caught off guard or surprised. We cannot be victorious against the forces of darkness that rule our world without the precise, perfect plans of the Lord. We need more books like this one! *Use this book as a spiritual tool to help teach the generations how to agree prophetically over what God has said. Use this book as you redefine your mind-set for walking in victory.* Believe that you can defeat your enemy! See your enemy. See his headship broken over your life. Do not be afraid to discover how his voice has ruled your bloodline. Remember Jesus! The Cross broke the headship of Satan. Drive a stake through his headship and you will begin to hear what God has for your future. Never forget that you have been given the ability to connect heaven and earth. Let the Lord teach you to pray today, "Thy will in heaven, come to earth!"

Barbara Yoder's *Taking On Goliath* is a defining document for this season!

—CHUCK D. PIERCE
PRESIDENT, GLORY OF ZION INTERNATIONAL MINISTRIES, INC.

Foreword

THE TRUTHS FOUND WITHIN THIS BOOK WILL BLESS your heart as they have blessed mine. Barbara Yoder has blessed the body of Christ with revelation and a challenge to the saints to be the warrior generation. If you have a desire to demonstrate to the world that there is no God comparable to our Lord Jesus Christ, then the truth in this book will make you free and the warrior spirit will be activated within you.

I have been a bishop to Barbara for many years, and she has served for many years as one of my board of governors. Apostle Barbara has pioneered and built a very successful church while at the same time traveling to the nations of the world. She is in great demand as a conference speaker, one who does not speak just from book learning but from fighting many personal and corporate battles for the church and nations.

There is an in-depth knowledge of the Word of God and spiritual warfare within Barbara. She is a woman of God with great integrity in her walk with the Lord and in her relationships with others. You can feel free to receive from her spirit as well as from the words written, for she is doctrinally sound and spiritually holy with a pure heart.

This book is a must-read for every Christian. It is absolutely essential that the saints become the militant, aggressive army of the Lord in this day and hour. Those who successfully fulfill the will of God will learn to properly use their spiritual weapons of warfare. In my books *The Eternal Church* and *Apostles, Prophets and the Coming Moves of God*, I reveal that God is raising up an army, not just an audience.

In the year 2008, the third and final apostolic reformation is being launched. Each reformation has several movements within it. The present reformation will have three: the saints movement, the army of the Lord movement, and the kingdom-establishing movement.

We must become warriors for our personal victories, prosperity, and successful ministry. As warriors we will be more effective in destroying the works of the devil and bringing God's kingdom to this world. Barbara is much younger than me, but, like myself, she is at that Moses stage of maturity and ministry. We both want to raise up Joshua leaders who will lead the younger generation in the military campaign to possess our promised Canaan land. The warrior generation is predestined to destroy the principalities over cities, nations, and kingdoms until the kingdoms of this world become the kingdom of our Lord Jesus and His church.

The Bible declares that our God is a mighty man of war, and His sons and daughters have His DNA. (See Exodus 15:3; Isaiah 42:13.) Yes, Jesus is a loving Savior, baptizer, healer, and deliverer, but He is also a powerful warrior who fights for His people.

Barbara's primary biblical illustration is David the worshiping warrior. As a youth he went to battle against the mighty giant Goliath. When he became king of Israel, he went to war against all who were in the land that God had promised to Abraham. David and his army killed hundreds of thousands of the enemy and expanded the kingdom of Israel to its prophesied borders. The New Testament calls David a man after God's own heart (Acts 13:22). If we are going to be a person with God's own heart, then we must be a worshiper of God and a mighty warrior for Jesus Christ.

There are more than enough scriptures and biblical examples in this book to convince any conscientious Christian that he or she has the right and responsibility to be a warrior in God's army. Only the overcoming warriors are promised a place of rulership in God's eternal kingdom. (See Revelation 20:6; 22:5.)

This book will be instrumental in fulfilling the desire of Christ Jesus to raise up an army of militant, aggressive warriors who will follow their commander in chief (Jesus) into the battles that must be won before Christ can return to Earth. May you hear what the Spirit is saying to the church and become one with the warrior generation.

—Dr. Bill Hamon
Bishop, Christian International Ministries Network

1

A Rude Awakening

I WAS FLYING FROM DETROIT TO NEWARK, AND THEN from Newark to Tel Aviv. The plane, a small commuter jet, left the Detroit gate on time. That was a victory, I thought, knowing the reputation of small commuter planes, which are notorious for being late or grounded because of weather or mechanical problems. I take them only when there is no other option.

This was going to be my first trip to Israel. I was excited to go in spite of the fact that my internal video screen was totally blank where Israel was concerned. I had never been anywhere in the Middle East; it was a big unknown to me. All I knew was that I wanted to meet the people of Israel and to figure out why God had placed that nation so deeply on my heart. (I'll explain later how the Holy Spirit reached into my heart and "hijacked" it for Israel.)

I was about to see everything I had only read about before. Little did I know I was also about to become a giant-killer.

MAKING CONNECTIONS

I should have known things were going awry when we proceeded toward a runway using the most obscure route possible. I fly out of Detroit all the time, so I have gotten to know the runways, terminals, gates, and planes like the back of my hand. When we arrived at this out-of-the-way location near the runway, which I had never noticed before, the pilot of the plane braked, turned off the engines, and waited.

Finally the pilot came on the speaker system to inform us that Newark air controllers had instructed us not to take off yet because there was too much congestion at the Newark airport. We would need to wait until more space was available in the air traffic flow. They did not know how long this would take.

More than an hour and twenty minutes later, we proceeded toward Newark. The flight attendant assured me that we would arrive in time to make our connections. My original connection time had been ninety minutes, which would have been more than adequate. According to our new estimated time of arrival, however, it was now reduced to ten minutes.

I could not understand how they had arrived at those numbers, but I figured they knew something I didn't. I began to compute the time in my mind anyway.

First, after getting off the plane, I would have to wait for my carry-on bag to be retrieved from the belly of the commuter jet. That would leave me with maybe five minutes to make it to the other gate, which I knew would take at least ten minutes.

Bingo! It did not take a rocket scientist to figure it out—I have just missed my plane.

Never fear; assurance is always near! There were at least three of us who were bound for the connecting Tel Aviv flight on Continental Airlines. The flight attendant kept reassuring us that someone with a cart would meet us at the gate and drive us to the other gate. She said we could go right out, catch the cart, and proceed to the other gate; then she would personally expedite the removal of our carry-on luggage from the belly of the plane, bring it to our departure gate, and deliver it to us in our seats.

Raise another red flag! No flight attendant ever personally delivers anyone's bags to a connecting flight. I noticed that none of the other connecting passengers bought her offer either.

In Newark, we deplaned as quickly as possible. Grabbing our carry-ons, we ran to find the cart just outside the Jetway. The cart was there, but there was no driver. I asked the desk clerk, "Where's the driver?" She said he had come and then left the cart to go do something.

Go *do* something? Now the writing on the wall was plain: *I am missing my connection.*

I could see through the window to the other side of the terminal. There it was, the giant airbus, pulling away to take off for Tel Aviv.

Despite my frustration level, I released a sigh of relief, thinking, "Well, at least my connection woes are over. I'll check with the service desk, and they'll give me a seat on the next plane."

Simple and straightforward, right? Wrong. Even so, I took my place in line for the next customer service agent.

When my turn came, everything broke loose. I was informed that I would now have to pay more than $2,000—in addition to my ticket that I already paid for—because I was currently booking a "new" flight. I would have to pay the price of the ticket as if I had just bought it today.

I tried to be nice at first. I really did! Then I just gave up. I let that agent have it.

The place became a war zone, almost slipping over into armed conflict; it was a war of words. I suddenly understood what people mean by road rage. I also understood how easily interpersonal conflicts can give rise to violence. I understood world wars, all kinds of wars. I was at war with anyone who got near me. I felt like I had just changed into battle fatigues and pulled out my arsenal.

At last, totally exasperated, I ended up in the Presidents Club lounge, where the staff intervened on my behalf. Now I could take off my fatigues, lay down my weapons, and become a normal, law-abiding citizen again. I was just an ordinary, nice Christian trying to be like Jesus. But it hadn't been this hard in a long, long time.

I had been so angry that now I wondered if I needed to get saved all over again. So I called the most spiritual friend I could remember and confessed my faults. With that taken care of I felt good again, clean and clear—and I had a fresh plane ticket in my hand as well.

I thought the war was over. Little did I know it was just beginning.

HIJACKED

Upon arrival in Tel Aviv, I stayed in a hotel for a couple of nights before leaving on the tour. We proceeded to the Sea of Galilee and the Golan Heights, where we stayed for a few more days. From there we headed on the last leg of our journey to Jerusalem. We were going to enter Jerusalem by traveling a back route up the Mount of Olives. The guide chronicled all the well-known historical sites that we passed as we ascended the mountain.

I should mention that several years earlier, at the annual November worship conference of the church I pastor, something unusual had happened to me. Just a month earlier, Jane Hansen Hoyt, president of Aglow International, told me about God "hijacking" her heart for the nation of Israel.

At the time I thought, "That's nice. I pray for the peace of Jerusalem out of obedience to the Word, but my heart has never been captured like that." I knew I had intellectual knowledge about the need to pray for Jerusalem, but I did not have revelation knowledge. I started to feel that I was on the outside of something I needed to be on the inside of.

Listening to Jane, an inward cry began to go up:

Lord, hijack my heart too! Let Jerusalem become more than head knowledge to me. Let it become a revelation!

After that conversation and prayer, I went about my ordinary activities for a month. Then at the worship conference, two people at two different times, unknown to each other, prophesied to me about Israel. During the second prophecy, I was overcome in an unusual way, overwhelmed on behalf of Israel and the Jewish people. It had happened. I had been arrested by God. I began to weep uncontrollably for the land and the people.

Robert and Ana Stearns were with me. I took Ana, who is Jewish, on my lap as if she were Israel, and I wept and prayed over that nation.

I knew that Israel was in the center of God's End Time plans. I knew that the time of the Gentiles would come to an end, and then it would be Israel's time. I also knew that Islam was at the core of this battle and that the whole Middle East would become the focal point of the world, with Jerusalem at the center. But I had no genuine comprehension of the magnitude of the importance of this city in the End Time conflict of the ages. And still, although I expected Jerusalem to become the focal point of the whole world, it remained vague in my mind.

I would have to go there in order to comprehend more fully. Now somehow Israel had been etched indelibly on the inner workings of my heart and mind, becoming a passion of my heart. Whereas I had never before had a desire to visit Israel, now I did.

Those are the events that led up to my present trip. I rehearsed them as we crept our way up a back route of the Mount of Olives.

Panorama

Suddenly we were at the top! I climbed out of the van, and the wind tore at me, howling. It seemed as if some sort of unseen storm had made itself at home there, settling on and surrounding that particular mountain, bringing with it a collage of emotional and spiritual sensory experiences.

The clouds scattered across the sky were angry looking. To me it was as if someone had painted a symbolic picture of the land's coexistence with war and peace. I felt I was viewing a spiritual war, a conflict of incomprehensible dimensions.

From where I was standing on this Mount of Olives, overlooking the heart of the city of Jerusalem, I could see Mount Moriah rising up in the midst of it. What did I see on the top of that mountain? The Islamic mosque of the Temple Mount—a potent symbol of the opposite force.

With my own eyes I was seeing the scope and sweep of the conflict. This was Jerusalem, center of my Christian roots, the place David conquered when he overcame the Jebusites, the pivotal control center of the Jewish and Christian world—long ago invaded and still occupied by an idolatrous religious structure. Here in the middle of Jerusalem sat a contrary force, a power structure contending for the control of not only the city of Jerusalem but also, ultimately, of the whole world. Before my eyes two kingdoms were conspicuously locked in conflict.

I found myself standing there in the violent wind, weeping uncontrollably. This was no ordinary emotional reaction. I was in travail for Israel, for the Jewish people, and for Christians around the world.

A desperate cry rose from the depths of my being: "Wake up!" It was a plea for the veil of deception to be removed from the hearts of Muslims. It was an entreaty for my own people, Christians, to awaken to the fact that war is in our midst.

Besides the sights (and sites), I became aware of actual, physical sounds. The Islamic call to prayer blared forth, sounding out across the valley to the top of the mountain and forcing its way into the airwaves.

I wanted to cover my ears. Right here in the open, multiplied hundreds of times, was the shrill sound of an anti-Semitic, antichrist, demonic structure that was vying for control. I comprehended, as never before, the size and scope of this religious war.

Now I knew why I had to come to Israel, to Jerusalem. No other place portrays as clearly the battle of the ages. Here the war was obvious, blatant, and playing itself out in a daily struggle not only for the land but also for the very atmosphere. I was standing in the middle of it, reeling to and fro as the kingdom of darkness warred against the kingdom of God. I rehearsed a familiar passage from the Book of Ephesians:

> For our struggle is not against flesh and blood, but against the rulers, against the powers, against the world forces of this darkness, against the spiritual forces of wickedness in the heavenly places. Therefore, take up the full armor of God, so that you will be able to resist in the evil day, and having done everything, to stand firm.
>
> —Ephesians 6:12–13, nas

With a rush of knowing and revelation, I understood Israel, the Jews, the sound, the religious spirit, and the conflict of the End

Times as never before. I could not stop weeping with gut-wrenching travail.

Part of it was weeping for my own history of not seeing, not knowing, not comprehending what was going on. Here I was leading a church congregation, yet we were only vaguely aware of the degree and intensity of the war involving the church at large. So I also wept over the Christian church in America, which is so far removed both physically and revelationally from the conflict.

In a moment of time, I had glimpsed and perceived the sweep of the struggle in the Middle East, and I had seen the antichrist spirit—a giant, a true Goliath. I had seen the prince of Persia dancing on the head of Jerusalem.

WHICH IS MORE REAL?

When I was growing up, my mother, who was very good and godly, loved *Better Homes and Gardens* magazine. So did her friends. I would page through her copies, dreaming about what my life would be like when I grew up.

I would be married, of course, and I would be the ideal mother of several children. We would all be healthy and cheerful, and we would live in a comfortable, pleasant home in a pretty, well-tended neighborhood full of gracious and helpful neighbors. Every day I would prepare delicious meals for my family. And as they devoured my homemade pies and cakes, we would all love and praise God.

With the freedom and simplicity of a carefree childhood, I went to the park, played in the sandbox, and enjoyed picnics. I gathered cherry blossoms (and cherries) from my favorite tree, picked flowers in May, and took little excursions on a grassy path to a hidden pond full of big goldfish. I swam in the lake and sometimes spent the afternoon in a canoe paddled by adults as we explored the lake's countless channels. The *Better Homes and Gardens* view of life established itself securely in my head as the model of the way life should be.

Having been raised in an evangelical Christian home and in an evangelical community, I grew up around many well-known missionaries and ministers, hearing their stories of sacrifice and conflict. This created some tension in my ideal universe. I knew people who had been prisoners of war during the Korean War; I heard firsthand stories about times of near-starvation when supper for several people had been one rat boiled in water. I was inspired by stories of those who trekked off to the jungle where there were no Christians, some of whom became martyrs in the process.

The stories were compelling, capturing my thinking. I wanted to do these types of things too; yet, I held on to my idealistic picture of my future. Needless to say, I needed to become much more mature in my approach to life. One scripture says:

> When I was a babe, as a babe I was speaking, as a babe I was thinking, as a babe I was reasoning, and when I have become a man, I have made useless the things of the babe.
>
> —1 CORINTHIANS 13:11, YLT

I needed to comprehend that life would never turn out the way I wanted it to be because *Better Homes and Gardens* is not reality. Eventually I would need to come face-to-face with giants, modern-day Goliaths. It would have to happen more than once because there would always be more than one Goliath. I would see him on the evening news and also in my own heart, house, and neighborhood. After many years, I would see with my own eyes one of the biggest Goliaths of all—the Middle East Goliath.

Battle Call

Yes, Goliath is all too real, and he is before us. We are in a war. This calls for a generation of warriors who will be inducted into a holy army, the army of God.

A rudimentary definition of the word *warrior* is "one who makes war." After a series of battles or conflicts, the man or woman who is a warrior can be considered a "seasoned warrior."

A warrior does not necessarily revel in the conflict itself, but rather in the goal of liberation. In *The Lord of the Rings*, J. R. R. Tolkien wrote: "I do not love the bright sword for its sharpness, nor the arrow for its swiftness, nor the warrior for his glory. I love only that which they defend."[1]

In this day, God is calling forth a formidable army of warriors, an entire generation. It is not limited to only one age group. It is a church generation made up of believers from all age groups and backgrounds who happen to be alive at the same time in these first decades of the twenty-first century.

This army infiltrates behind enemy lines, and it perseveres for as long as it takes to win. This army is ordinary people doing extraordinary and supernatural feats under the command of God Himself. In other words, this generation is a *chosen* generation. As Peter put it:

> You are a chosen generation, a royal priesthood, a holy nation,
> His own special people, that you may proclaim the praises of
> Him who called you out of darkness into His marvelous light.
> —1 Peter 2:9

A chosen generation is willing to be inducted into the army of God. A chosen warrior generation is willing to be transformed into whatever

God needs them to be. Not only do they abandon their *Better Homes and Gardens* mentality, but they also lay down their ideas of what the battle consists of. Paul beseeched his readers:

> Therefore I urge you, brethren, by the mercies of God, to present your bodies a living and holy sacrifice, acceptable to God, which is your spiritual service of worship. And do not be conformed to this world, but be transformed by the renewing of your mind…
>
> —ROMANS 12:1–2, NAS

We are not meant to look like the rest of our culture, age group, or racial profile; we are to be transformed. We are not meant to be a generation defined by the world; we are meant to be the chosen generation of God, resembling Him and following Him. He is a multigenerational God—"I am the God of Abraham, Isaac, and Jacob" (Exod. 3:6; Matt. 22:32; Mark 12:26; Acts 7:32). He looks at us in the context of our rebirth into His kingdom. Therefore, whether we are teenagers or old enough to stand on the threshold of heaven, we are part of *His* generation.

This generation of warriors is called to face off with the Goliaths of the world and the Goliaths of the culture. This generation is a Davidic company because it was David who faced off with Goliath and overcame the enemies of God.

GENERATION

Generations generate. They produce offspring—physically, intellectually, emotionally, and spiritually.

Whatever it is, it is an act of procreation. Procreation implies multiplication, which is the process of bringing about more of something.

If you are a businessperson, you generate results, you look at numbers (e.g., customers, products, income), and you want to continue to see your business grow.

The chosen generation is supposed to produce the offspring of God. We are supposed to produce fruit that looks and acts like God, whether that consists of individuals or activities. Basic to Scripture is the idea that every single one of us is the seed for the next generation of seed.

The next generation will resemble this one, and every generation has been ordered, aligned, and assigned by the living God, who sets the times and seasons. That means it is no mistake that you and I are alive right now. This is exciting!

God has ordained and aligned a warrior generation for this age, and He wants that generation to bring forth results. He wants us to yield the new kingdom harvest that will overtake the old and evil one.

How do we respond to this? How do we reframe our understanding?

One way is through prayer. Not just "God bless" prayers, but prophetic prayers. Those who pray these prayers hear God and then apostolically declare the Word of the Lord over people, situations, and nations. God has called you and me—ordinary people—to confound the world, because He is a holy God who possesses us as mighty warriors and leads us forward into victory.

> Take a good look, friends, at who you were when you got called into this life. I don't see many of "the brightest and the best" among you, not many influential, not many from high-society families. Isn't it obvious that God deliberately chose men and women that the culture overlooks and exploits and abuses,

chose these "nobodies" to expose the hollow pretensions of the "somebodies"?

—1 Corinthians 1:26–28, The Message

Have you already enlisted in this army? Goliath is getting to his feet. He has you in his sights. Time is running out. Will you join me?

2

Waking Up With Goliath

I AM THE SENIOR PASTOR OF A CHURCH IN Michigan, and I frequently travel to speak at churches and conferences around the world. A few months ago I was preparing for a trip where I was to speak at a major conference. I was expected to have a significant word of direction or wisdom, something for the nation that would equip warriors in their battles with the forces of darkness.

But I wasn't prepared. My mind was a million miles away. Because of a combination of situations, I was anxious, worried, and apprehensive. I felt frantic and panicked to the point of emotional paralysis. In that state, I did not care what happened to the nation; I was consumed with finding some way through my own maze of tangled, strangling thoughts. I could not find my way out of being absolutely shut up and shut down in a valley of despair.

Things only got worse. The more I tried to think about what I was going to say at this conference, the more my mind locked up and my emotions went haywire. My chest felt as if there were tight bands around it. My brain felt like it was going to explode and splatter against the wall. The more I tried to get myself under control, the more I found myself out of control.

I tried everything.

I read the Bible to myself; silently at first, then aloud, and using every translation I had. That didn't seem to work.

I began to sing every praise song I could think of. I sang hymns. I put worship music in my CD player and turned up the volume so high that it rocked the house. I love music, and music usually works, but not this time. This time I only got more aggravated, more annoyed, more irritated, and ultimately more hopeless.

I prayed silently. I prayed aloud. Then I just prayed really loud—so loud that I think my neighbors could probably hear me with both their windows and mine closed. I prayed in English. I prayed in the Spirit. None of that worked.

So I tried kneeling down. I hadn't knelt down to pray in a long time; I usually stood or walked around. I thought that if I knelt down, maybe God would see how intent I was to reach Him and how desperately I needed to break through the war that was gripping me. It still didn't seem to help.

Then I stood back up. I paced. I knelt again. I yelled, "Help!" None of it worked.

My mind searched desperately for something that would bring a breakthrough. I thought maybe it was because of sin. Had I committed some sin I wasn't aware of? Was God hiding from me because of it? I asked God if I had disappointed Him in some area of my life. The next thing I know, a horde of facts descended on me, condemning me. It felt as if all of hell had moved in to keep me company. In fact, the horde even crawled into bed with me so that I could not sleep.

Now I was in an even greater emotional mess than I had been in the first place. On top of the already difficult situation, I had just piled on a mountain of self-accusations. I was buried under all of the reasons I would never move forward. I might as well have called and asked the local garbage company to come and dump their week's worth of garbage on my front lawn because it was there already—invisible to others, but not to me.

I realized that my mind was in such a state that I could only perceive the negative. In fact, I was displaying an amazing ability to turn any positive into a negative, almost instantly. This was suspicious. Finally I began to realize that I was up against something. What was that something? At that point, I recognized my Goliath.

AUTHORITY OVER PHILISTINES

I began to think about Goliath, and I began to think about David. I began to think about the Philistines and Israel. Soon I was reading and rehearsing the entire state of affairs in 1 Samuel 17, and I realized that there was a reason *this* Goliath was before me—*this* Goliath who was not only irritating me but also terrifying me.

I knew if I could find a way to overcome my current situation, this personal Goliath, I would be better equipped to help others overcome theirs. I would have earned the legal spiritual authority over Goliaths that are both personal and corporate. Not only would I step into this new authority, but I would also discover new wisdom and strategies for overcoming insurmountable obstacles.

I turned the pages of my Bible back to the beginning of 1 Samuel 17—the story of David and Goliath—to see what relevance that confrontation has for me (and for you) today.

The first thing I saw was that it was really David's public debut as a warrior. He had warred before, defeating both a bear and a lion when they came to attack his flock of sheep. But those instances happened with no one else watching him. Those early battles occurred in private.

That corresponded to many of my battles, and it made me ask myself,

"Where have I fought the enemy and won the battle when no one could see? Where have I become an overcomer in the secret, hidden places when no one was looking?"

You and I have to become overcomers in the secret, hidden places of our lives before God will bring us out into the open. What are you doing when no one else is looking? How are you letting God develop you? Are you being responsible and accountable for your life? Are you paying the price for the mantle that God wants you to carry?

Part of the price that you have to pay so that you can carry the presence and power, as well as gift of God, to the people around you is the hiddenness price, the humility price. You have to be willing to work as David did, without recognition.

David started with sheep. I hope you know that sheep are among the dumbest animals of all. My little puppy is probably smarter than the smartest sheep. And, besides that, they stink.

Sheep need the shepherd for everything. They cannot find their own way. They can't even get back up if they fall down.

That's what young, strong, handsome David had been stuck with—a flock of stupid sheep. He was not allowed to help with the family hunting or anything that would have seemed a little manlier. He was stuck, by himself, taking care of a flock of the dumbest animals in creation. He probably ended up smelling like them, and he had no one to talk to. (The sheep weren't much company. They just complained and cried all day long, "Baa, baa, baa…")

But was David willing to take risks for his father's sheep?

You bet.

Was he willing to give his life for the sheep?

Yes, he was.

This became one of the marks of a true warrior. In one of David's early battles, he had taken on a bear single-handedly, not knowing if he would come out of the conflict alive. In his next battle, again single-handedly, David didn't hesitate to defend his sheep against a lion, even though he could have been maimed. He took them on in order to defend his father's sheep.

How did he do it? Through the skilled use of his slingshot—David practiced and trained during his long hours of watching over the flock, and, when he needed to use his weapon, he was prepared. David had endured the endless days and nights of boredom in his life as a shepherd. He had developed perseverance as a result.

Furthermore, David knew that worship was a secret to strength. The joy of the Lord was His strength. So he had also spent much of that boring downtime writing songs and singing them to God. In other words, he had developed the dimensions of his character and balanced his personal desires with godly ones.

Little did he know how much he was going to need that long-staying power when he became Israel's king. The long war between Saul and David, in itself, would be enough of a reason to need that firm character foundation.

You and I find ourselves in long, drawn-out conflicts too. We aren't in a little war anymore. Is it any wonder that we find ourselves up against personal odds? God is preparing us to face bigger battles and to win more significant fields. When we get there and identify the giant Goliath who is standing in the field, our slingshot and our warrior character need to be ready.

MANIFESTATIONS OF EVIL

Our Goliaths birth us into a whole new arena of authority. They sit at the entrance gates to a new and expanded sphere of authority and influence.

In my book *The Breaker Anointing*, I wrote about the demonic structures that sit at the entrance to a new place.[1] They are there to intimidate you and me. They are there to make us waver and to threaten us with death. This evil power is trying to keep us in our old place of defeat or at least in a former arena of authority. This power must be overcome.

After David overcame Goliath, he was given a new place of kingdom recognition by Saul as well as the people. His victory transformed the way his family saw him. No longer was he merely the youngest of many sons, a smelly shepherd boy. Now he was a warrior.

If you have ever wondered why you have faced so many tests, so many "giants" who are like Goliaths in your life, it's because God is making a warrior out of you. He is preparing you for new and expanded places of authority and influence. As you overcome your personal Goliaths, you can face bigger ones in the public arena. It's called *earned authority*.

Crystal Hamon, the granddaughter of Bishop Bill and Evelyn Hamon, is a young woman who understands this principle. She contributed some thoughts for this chapter:

> My grandparents can tell you where they were the day President John F. Kennedy was shot, and so can most people who were alive at the time. These days, people swap stories of their experiences on the day the twin towers fell. But both of our generations had been marked by global war long before these dark, historic days.

This war is one of a powerful, destructive, and subtle nature. Our fight is deeply spiritual. Even if you've never described it this way out loud, chances are you feel its effects. The assaults descend from multiple directions and are aimed at our hearts. The wounds strike our bodies, our intellects, our relationships, and, most deeply, our souls. The turmoil of these struggles on an individual level then spreads like sickness throughout our social networks and leadership structures.

The motives are not new: steal, kill, and destroy. The weapons are always the same: shame, fear, violence, poverty, control, perversion, greed, ignorance, addiction, disease, and so on. Some may call these manifestations of evil in our generation nothing more than human weaknesses, but Paul warned us not to be ignorant of the enemy's scheming devices (2 Cor. 2:11). Once they are identified as spiritual opponents, we can fight them with the weapons God provides.

Many people in the church have rediscovered the arsenal of God. Fighting men and women are dusting off armaments like prayer, fasting, humility, and intercession. They are uncovering the power of loving the people who have made themselves their enemies. They are learning about hearing the voice of God and communing with their Creator and His family in the presence of their enemies. This warrior generation is learning how they have already been given power over the enemy and how to enforce that authority.

I was brought up in a family who taught me how to use some of these weapons. I had spiritual dreams and a heightened sensitivity to spiritual things. In my childhood, there were times when I dealt with intense anxiety. I didn't know what it was; I only knew that I would suddenly feel horribly afraid and sick to my stomach.

One day I remember walking down the hallway in my house, and suddenly, like a wave out of nowhere, this feeling gripped me. In the same moment, I realized that this was nothing more than a spiritual attack, which I had been given authority over. So I stopped and commanded anxiety to bow its knee to the authority of Jesus Christ.

Instantly, I was flooded with peace. I knew I had found the key to winning that particular battle. I also knew that I would be called to fight bigger battles because I was getting lots of practice fighting personal, spiritual attacks.

KEY LESSONS FROM DAVID

In facing off with Goliaths, there are some key lessons to learn. Here are some of the keys I found as I studied 1 Samuel 17:

The enemy sets up many battlefronts.

First Samuel 17:1 states, "Now the Philistines gathered their armies together to battle, and were gathered together at Sochoh, which belongs to Judah; they encamped between Sochoh and Azekah, in Ephes Dammim." This verse says the Philistines "gathered their armies." There was not just one army; not just one, isolated place experiencing war.

In Hebrew the word *Philistine* means "rolling, up and down, migratory, changing geographical positions, rolling in dust or wallowing in self."[2] Philistines battle against their enemies on several fronts at one time. When they battle, they change tactics; they "roll up and down." They come to devour their foes, to "eat their lunch," to feed on them, to overcome them, and to prevail over them.

Think about how this applies to the situation I described at the beginning of this chapter. I found that I was up against a Goliath, and Goliath was a Philistine. In a Philistine experience, the enemy will be migratory. He will show up at one place one day and another place the next day. It is extremely difficult to locate the enemy's position because he does not remain stationary.

If I do not know where my enemy is going to show up next, it's impossible for me to know how to position myself. That's why I was up one day, one hour, one moment, and then down the next. A Philistine experience feels like a roller-coaster ride, and a wild one at that!

In addition, Philistines roll us in dust. In more contemporary language, they drag us through the dirt. Any dirt a Philistine can find, he will roll you in.

That's what happened to me. I felt like I must have done something wrong somewhere, somehow. I felt there must have been some sin—dirt—I couldn't locate that had caused God to turn against me. I rehearsed every mistake, failure, and shortcoming I could think of.

This can look different for each person, depending on the situation. Perhaps you have spent or invested your money in a way that now seems totally wrong or ignorant. Perhaps you bought a house and then you lost your job and couldn't pay the mortgage. Perhaps your spouse turned on you for no reason at all, and now he or she is freely informing everyone of your stupidity. Perhaps someone reminds you of something you did wrong years ago that you have already asked forgiveness for.

On top of rolling you in dirt, Philistines will make you wallow in your *self.* Self-pity comes along and sets up residence in your house. You think, "Woe is me." And you start believing the worst. You believe "bad" is going to happen any minute.

What can you use to help you forget it all? A movie or novel? Valium, Prozac, alcohol, or drugs? Another business deal? Sex? You feel you are a complete failure—always have been and always will be. You are convinced that you are not as smart, good-looking, etc. as everyone else.

You begin to think like Alexander in a favorite children's book, who said, "I went to sleep with gum in my mouth and now there's gum in my hair and when I got out of bed this morning, I tripped on my skateboard and by mistake I dropped my sweater in the sink while the water was running and I could tell it was going to be a terrible, horrible, no good, very bad day!"[3]

The battle finally becomes so wearisome that you give in to desperation, exasperation, helplessness, and hopelessness. "There is nothing I can do. I can't overcome this thing. It is over. I will now throw in the towel."

Goliath is a Philistine.

Not only did David have to go out against the Philistine armies, but he also had to go out against a specific Philistine named Goliath. In the same way, we can only become a warrior by means of a specific Goliath. Ours may be a Goliath of illness or of poverty, a Goliath of humanistic thinking or sexual impurity. Whatever it is, it will loom big compared to our puny stature.

Goliath was a *giant* of a man: "A champion went out from the camp of the Philistines, named Goliath, from Gath, whose height was six cubits and a span" (1 Sam. 17:4). This translates into more than nine feet tall. He was considered a champion, which means that not only was he a man of impressive size, but he was also a winner. He was used to prevailing over his opponents. He was proud of his strength and his prowess.

So David volunteered to take Goliath out, something that nobody else had dared to do. He couldn't get the Philistines to substitute some other warrior, and he couldn't go out as part of the army his brothers were fighting with. Here he had been on an ordinary errand from his father—"go take lunch to your brothers"—and the next thing he knows, he's taking on Goliath single-handedly.

The same thing happens to us. We think we're on an ordinary errand, and all of a sudden the enemy looms up in our face. We hardly have time to think. David didn't.

The army of Israel was terribly afraid of the Philistines, and especially of Goliath. (See 1 Samuel 17:24.) But not David.

Instead of running for cover, David was attracted to the challenge. His perspective was quite different from the perspective of the other men in Israel. All of the other men were overcome by the problem. They talked to one another about the problem, fellowshiped over the problem, talked the problem into the ground, scared each other with the problem, and repeated the problem over and over. There was only one who stood up and said, "Who is this uncircumcised Philistine, that he should defy the armies of the living God?" (1 Sam. 17:26).

Everyone knew that David was someone with a different nature. He wasn't down wallowing in the mud and dirt because of the enemy's threats. He was not overcome by the demonic power before him. Davids are not scared off by Philistines. When they see a Goliath, something rises up inside them and they challenge the giant. They take up where the last giant-killer left off.

This generation of godly men and women that you and I are a part of is doing the same thing. We have been challenged from all directions by Philistine giants. Instead of mulling over the problem as the Israelites did, we need to become Davids. Instead of sitting around having seminars about a problem, we need to be people who see a Goliath and burst out with, "Oh boy! Let me at him! I have a solution!"

We don't get depressed, and we don't wallow in the dirt. Instead, we get energized. It's part of the Davidic personality to rise to the challenge of the battlefield, even when we thought we were just taking lunch to our brothers. It's as if we're made for this challenge.

Davids rule in the midst of their foes.

The Philistines secured positions in Judah, in Israel's homeland. In the same way, they also take up positions inside of you and me. They invade our minds, emotions, wills, and physical bodies. The longer they remain in their positions on our inside territory, the more afraid we become. We become confused and sick.

This is what they want. They are there to terrify us. They are there to make us give up. But we are warriors, so we won't.

There they are, setting up their enemy camps in the midst of Judah. (*Judah* is Hebrew for "praise.") That is one primary way we rule in the midst of our enemies, through praising God.

At first, we may feel as if the very thing that has enabled us to overcome in the past has now been taken from us because we open our mouths, but nothing comes out. We can't do it; we can't even offer up a sacrifice of praise. (See Jeremiah 33:11; Hebrews 13:15.)

But then something changes. Judah's patriarchal blessing states:

> Judah, you are he whom your brothers shall praise;
> Your hand shall be on the neck of your enemies;
> Your father's children shall bow down before you.
> —GENESIS 49:8

To grab someone's neck with your hand is to keep that person's head from being able to move. Therefore the person can't talk; they can't fight or do anything. Just as taking someone by the neck paralyzes the command center of that person's body, Judah (praise) paralyzes the command center of the enemy.

Even if the enemy has already set up his military positions in Judah, in the midst of our praises, we will be able to overthrow him—although it will be difficult. After all, he is on our territory; he has captured our praises. We have to let them loose before we can begin to prevail.

Here's how you can start praising and prevailing. Understand that biblically, praise is always verbal. In other words, it's a spoken-aloud action. So to reestablish your footing of praise, simply open your Bible and begin to declare one of David's psalms aloud:

> Bless the LORD, O my soul;
> And all that is within me, bless His holy name!
> Bless the LORD, O my soul,
> And forget not all His benefits:
> Who forgives all your iniquities,
> Who heals all your diseases,
> Who redeems your life from destruction,
> Who crowns you with lovingkindness and tender mercies,
> Who satisfies your mouth with good things,
> So that your youth is renewed like the eagle's....
> But the mercy of the LORD is from everlasting to everlasting
> On those who fear Him,
> And His righteousness to children's children.
> —PSALM 103:1–5, 17

You can personalize this even more. Where are you sick right now? Put your hand wherever you have something wrong and say, "Who heals all my diseases." He heals every single one of them—my young-age diseases, my middle-age diseases, my old-age diseases, my genetic diseases, my nongenetic diseases, and the diseases of my fathers, my grandfathers, and my great-grandfathers. He clears out my arteries; He heals the muscles in my heart; He restores my lungs. He heals all of my diseases.

Say, "Bless the Lord, O my soul, because He has redeemed my life from destruction." He will not let the destroyer destroy you. You can say:

Destroyer, you have no authority. I'm beginning to get happy because my name is Judah, because I'm of the tribe of Judah. I'm of the line of David, and Jesus came out of David and out of Judah. I've been made to put my hand on the neck of the enemy. Destruction is going to cease. Sickness and disease are going to break off me. My head will be crowned with loving-kindness and tender mercies. God will satisfy me with good things so that my youth will be restored and renewed. I fear Him. I choose life, not death, so that my days will be long. I will have the length of life to come into my full inheritance.

GOD OF THE VALLEYS

When I was struggling against the Goliath I described at the beginning of this chapter, I felt I was in the deepest valley I had experienced in years. I forgot that it was in a valley that David met Goliath:

Saul and the men of Israel were gathered together, and they encamped in the Valley of Elah, and drew up in battle array against the Philistines. The Philistines stood on a mountain on one side, and Israel stood on a mountain on the other side, with a valley between them.

—1 SAMUEL 17:2–3

Goliath doesn't meet us when we're on a mountaintop. It doesn't take a rocket scientist to figure that out. He knows that when we're up there, we are in control and we're feeling strong. No, instead he meets us when we are at our lowest point, when we are vulnerable. He looks for the times when we are in a personal, family, church, or societal valley. He knows that's when he will have the advantage. He always aims for below the belt, at a most vulnerable place within us.

Consequently, it is while in the valley that we must overcome our enemy. Read this prophetic word delivered by Barbara Wentroble and Keith Pierce at Glory of Zion Church in Denton, Texas. This is a word that encourages us to stand up and fight the enemy, right where we are, in our current valley. It refers to the familiar story of the valley of dry bones in Ezekiel 37.[4]

> *Barbara Wentroble*: In days past you have learned that I am the God of the mountains. You have learned that I am a victorious God that conquers the mountain. You shall also know that I am Lord of the valley. The valley has seemed to pull you down, but I have put resurrection power within it.... You shall speak to the valley. You shall speak to the dead bones. You shall see the life of My Spirit come forth....

> *Keith Pierce*: In this valley place, look and see the dry bones around you. Begin to speak to those bones; speak to them clearly. Speak to them with the authority that I am giving you and you will begin to hear them rattle. When they rattle, they will begin to come together. When they come together, you will see what is dead brought to life in a new way.

> Do not let the valley capture you, but learn how to speak to your surroundings, because today is a day that I am awakening

the dry bones. Today is a day that the dry bones are being knitted together. Today is a day that what has been dead is coming to life in His holy name.

Barbara: Even as it was on the Day of Pentecost when I released tongues of fire upon My church, I shall once again release My fire upon My people. Your tongue shall be like that of a fire. It shall go forth with the word of the Lord. It shall burn up the enemy, and it shall ignite the people of God. I will take the very word that I have hidden in your heart; no longer shall it be a hidden word. It shall come forth as a mighty declaration of the power of God.

Receive a fresh fire that I am releasing upon you and know that the word that I have put within you shall not remain locked up. You shall release it in the same way that the Word of the Lord was released in the valley of dry bones where there was a supernatural manifestation of My power. Expect a supernatural manifestation of My power upon your word. Do not hold back, but release the Word of the Lord and watch the fire of God burn up your enemies.

Keith: Lift up your hands and receive the anointing. When the enemy arises, raise your anointed hand and see a supernatural release going out from your fingertips. It will turn back, bring down, and cast aside what the enemy has sent. I am God and I will turn what has been sent against My children back on the head of the evil one.

Barbara: Do not fear confrontation. In days past when there was a time of confrontation, you pulled back in fear and intimidation. This is a new season of courage. David stood in that moment as he faced Goliath; there was a time of divine confrontation. In this hour, I am going to take what I have put in your hand and use it against the enemy. You shall not fear confrontation. You shall not run from it, you shall run into it and you shall see the victory of the Lord.

Keith: Meet the confrontation like a storm because He rides in on the wind. When you meet it head on, you will see the wind of His Spirit released. His wind will clear a pathway, break down trees, and open up the way. He is coming through! He's coming through! He's coming through!

STRENGTH MADE PERFECT IN WEAKNESS

In the valley, the low place, we are intimidated, threatened, and knocked down, even panicky. And yet it was in the Valley of Elah that the Philistines were overcome. *Elah* means "oak tree, strength, chief, or mighty." In the valley, we can tap into strength that will withstand the enemy.

Oaks are massive trees that can stand strong and secure through storms, providing shelter. They grow in the valleys, not on the mountaintops. In what seems like the weakest place, oaks grow strong, and their strength can be manifested in us and through us.

Because of the extravagance of those revelations, and so I wouldn't get a big head, I was given the gift of a handicap to keep me in constant touch with my limitations. Satan's angel did his best to get me down; what he in fact did was push me to my knees. No danger then of walking around high and mighty! At first I didn't think of it as a gift, and begged God to remove it. Three times I did that, and then he told me, My grace is enough; it's all you need. My strength comes into its own in your weakness.

Once I heard that, I was glad to let it happen. I quit focusing on the handicap and began appreciating the gift. It was a case of Christ's strength moving in on my weakness. Now I take limitations in stride, and with good cheer, these limitations that cut me down to size—abuse, accidents, opposition, bad breaks. I just let Christ take over! And so the weaker I get, the stronger I become.

—2 CORINTHIANS 12:7–10, THE MESSAGE

In the valley, we will see our weakness turned into strength because God's strength is made perfect in our weakness.

3

Goliath Stands Before Us

WHEN I WAS ABOUT TEN, A NEIGHBOR FRIEND and I built a playhouse. One sunny, summer day, we took the cardboard box that my mother's new washer and dryer had come in, and we made it our own.

Our house was big, and it was strong. We were pretty proud of it. I remember cutting windows in our house, making a door, covering the floor with old blankets to simulate carpeting, and placing a very small "table" in there.

My friend and I moved in, spending whole days in our house. It was big enough so that we could invite our neighborhood friends to visit. Everyone was impressed—until it rained one day. We had one of those torrential storms, and, afterward, what did our big, strong playhouse look like? A crumpled pile of soggy cardboard, that's what.

We were devastated. We hadn't thought of that.

That cardboard house stands in my mind as a marker point. It's a constant reminder not to build houses out of cardboard, but rather to value the wisdom, understanding, and knowledge that come from God, as well as experience.

I have already chronicled other aspects of my idyllic childhood. Sheltered, I lived my early years in a very small town that also happened to be something of a national, evangelical summer capital. The most arduous activities I engaged in were swimming in the lake, eating ice cream bars and Eskimo pies, and sleeping under the benches in the sawdust-floored tabernacle. On warm and lazy summer days, I climbed my favorite cherry tree in our front yard and positioned myself on a huge limb to watch the world go by. By the hour, I played Monopoly with my friends.

All of that seems light-years removed from the realities of this present world.

Today, as Eamonn Kelly stated in his book *Powerful Times*, we are living in the best of times and the worst of times.[1] The future is far more complex, dangerous, and enigmatic than anything we have previously experienced in this nation. There is not a clear path from point A to point B anymore.

How do I perceive and evaluate this era? If I look too hard at the times through the world's eyes, everything appears to be intimidating and frightening. If I look at it from God's viewpoint, I see not only the challenges but also the great potential for the church. I can go back and forth. Some mornings when I wake up I want to start yelling like Chicken Little, "The sky is falling! The sky is falling!" Other days I say, "Everything will be all right."

You and I are completing the first decade of the twenty-first century. Whether we are prepared for it or even want to be here, this is our place, our assigned time, and our assignment lies before us. I don't know about you, but sometimes I have this surreptitious desire to become an ostrich and bury my head in the sand. Unlike David, who boldly went out and presented himself to his brothers, to Saul, and then to Goliath, I feel a bit less courageous.

Significant Goliaths are standing in front of us. These challenges are daunting. It is no accident of history that you and I are alive at this time— God wants to use us to shape the world in which He has placed us.

WISDOM, UNDERSTANDING, KNOWLEDGE

As challenging as the present seems to be, even more challenging years lie ahead of us—we have never needed God more than we do right now. Jesus Himself said that without God, we can do nothing. (See John 15:5.) In order to build His house, we need to have learned our "cardboard house" lessons. More than anything, we need His wisdom, His understanding, and His knowledge. A proverb in Scripture pulls these three words together:

> Through skillful and godly *Wisdom* is a house (a life, a home, a family) built, and by *understanding* it is established [on a sound and good foundation], and by knowledge shall its chambers [of every area] be filled with all precious and pleasant riches.
> —PROVERBS 24:3–4, AMP, EMPHASIS ADDED

These three characteristics—wisdom, understanding, knowledge— are vital to the building process. "The fear of the LORD is the beginning of wisdom, and the knowledge of the Holy One is understanding" (Prov. 9:10).

Wisdom starts with the fear of the Lord. He is our starting place. If I want wisdom, I must esteem Him more highly than any other source of wisdom.

Wisdom builds a house, a life, a home, a family. That can be expanded to include a neighborhood, a town, a city, a state, or a nation. Wisdom also builds a corporation, a university, a hospital, a government, a school system, a bank or economic system, a media network, a technology, and an artistic endeavor.

Understanding establishes the house. The word *understanding* includes reason, intelligence, skillfulness, and discretion. To understand is to comprehend or grasp the meaning of something. In school I memorized many things that I never understood. If I am to establish what I build on a solid foundation, I must understand *what* I am doing as well as *why* I am doing it.

Knowledge causes the house to be furnished. Knowledge is information: facts, ideas, truths, principles. Knowledge is both theoretical and practical, and we gain it through both study and personal experience, developing a familiarity with issues that concern not only our lives but also the world in which we live.

Anyone who builds something wants it to last long enough to accomplish its purpose. Ideally, the thing that is built will give rise to a subsequent generation, which understanding and knowledge will help to mature so that the next generation can carry on once the builder is gone.

Does the church build this way? Not very often.

It seems that much of the church is ignorant of what is going on in the world. As a result, it tends to build its future out of its past. The church always seems to be at least ten years behind the times, stuck in old ways of thinking. In other words, wisdom, understanding, and knowledge seem to be missing in the American church as we know it.

ASKING THE RIGHT QUESTIONS

To fully utilize wisdom, understanding, and knowledge, we must ask questions. Practically speaking, which questions should we ask to arrive at the answers we need?

To ask the right questions in the right spirit is even better. Jesus was always asking questions. His questions plumbed the depths of issues and got right to the heart of the matter. As a member of the warrior generation, consider the following:

- What are the key issues in this decade or era?
- Who or what is creating these issues?
- Whom do these issues affect?
- Where will these issues have their greatest influence or impact?
- What are the timelines? How soon will issues need to be faced and solved?
- How does the present prevailing reality affect the church and its mission? What are the implications for the church?
- What is God saying and doing in the midst of this world's reality?

For us the foundational question becomes, as Francis Schaeffer so aptly stated it in the title of his best-known book, *How Should We Then Live?*

The Church Is Changing

Could it be that what has worked in the past is no longer working because God is up to something? Could it be that God has intentionally created a hunger in His people through the absence of fulfillment, which catapults us into an unrelenting search for answers? Could it be that the answers to our dilemma can be found only through finding God in a whole new way?

We do seem to lose God if we devise programs and methods to fill the void of irrelevancy. Could it be that there are even ways we have been "doing church" that have become like a Goliath, an enemy to the ideal purposes of God?

The church itself seems to be changing these days. In an article in *Rev!* magazine, Alan Nelson wrote about the "Emergent church" movement. This movement is an attempt by evangelicals to change the church so that it can both understand and reach the culture. He made the following statement:

> I've tried to get my arms around this whole Church in emerging culture phenomenon. I've talked with those in the Emergent Movement, ingested a dozen books by those active in it, and attended several conferences on and for it. I'm convinced of three things:
>
> 1. Something significant is shifting.
> 2. Anyone who claims to know exactly what is happening is lying.
> 3. What's out there needs to be reckoned with if the Church in America is to have any relevance at all to culture.
>
> ...Besides its own internal issues, the Church has a lot to grapple with in the world at large. There are so many Goliaths, we don't know where to start. I have assembled a couple of lists of cultural trends and global threats just to get you thinking.[2]

CULTURAL TRENDS IN AMERICA

As a society, we have embraced relativism. In other words, people no longer accept single concepts of truth or the Bible itself as the source of absolute truth. Values have slipped. For example, sex is now OK as long as it occurs within the context of a committed relationship. Committed relationships have become the defining value rather than the biblical value of abstinence outside of a marriage—one man and one woman—relationship.[3]

Consider the following cultural trends, all of which have spiritual implications:

Absence of Christian beliefs

Just to take a slice of the population, according to one report, only 4 percent of teenagers in America are true Christians who have a personal relationship with Jesus Christ. Some teens have no clue as to what the cross on a church means. I heard Ron Luce, founder and president of Teen Mania Ministries, state that every Christian youth group in America would have to double every year for the next five years to reverse this trend.[4]

Pluralism

In terms of spiritual beliefs, pluralism means that there is no single path to God. Buddhism, Hinduism, New Age, or whatever someone thinks is "the way" will work as long as we end up with "god"—an ill-defined god at that. Pluralism rejects the Bible as the source of absolute truth. Many Americans prefer pluralism as the most plausible belief system.

In terms of human cultural mix, American culture is increasingly formed from multiple cultures. Hispanics or Latinos have emerged as the leading minority group, Latinizing the national culture. The Caucasian majority, who came from European roots, is aging and cannot compete with the fertility rates of the minorities. Asian and Middle Eastern nations are sending a flood of immigrants to American shores. This has a noticeable effect on the Judeo-Christian underpinnings of our national character.

The church, in some places, is waking up to the fact that God has brought the nations to us. Rather than viewing multiculturalism as a threat ("They're taking us over!"), the church is beginning to see this trend as an opportunity to evangelize more people. Visionary strategies allow the church to invade multiple religious structures in hopes of transforming the nations whose citizens have immigrated to our nation by first changing the hearts of the people.

Economic erosion

This one is not hard to see—it affects your pocketbook as well as mine. America has become dependent on Middle Eastern oil. Much of our food is imported. American manufacturing is increasingly taking place in other nations. As a result, we are at the mercy of other nations, and our economic system is staggering under the load. Our future is being undermined as a result. We are teetering on the brink of the most significant recession in recent times.

Spiritual curiosity

Growing alongside relativism and pluralism is an insatiable spiritual curiosity for anything "spiritual." Eastern religions have proliferated in the United States since the late 1960s. At some universities, shamanism is taught. Some corporations now have a "spiritual department" through which their employees' spirituality is nurtured. Of course, the term *spirituality* is very broadly defined to include all meaningful activities and relationships within the context of a higher power, including various forms of meditation, yoga, and prayer rooms.

Although church attendance is not tracking with population growth, spiritual interest is on the rise. Christianity as practiced in the church seems to have become irrelevant.

This sort of thing could paint a bleak picture of spirituality in

America except for the positive side: spiritual inquisitiveness and openness to the supernatural world creates a natural platform for the charismatic expression of the church and the experience of the gifts of the Holy Spirit. Therefore, never before have so many segments of our nation been more open to supernatural things.

Could this be an open door for those who understand the import of releasing the miraculous nature of God into the world? Jesus said, "My meat is to do the will of him that sent me, and to finish his work" (John 4:34, KJV). Is this "meat" for the warrior generation?

Sexualized culture

It seems as if there are no boundaries anymore. Adultery and fornication are rampant, not only in the society at large but in the church as well. Television and Internet ads are sexualized. Previous taboos have been eliminated, and television programs include sex acts.

It is now "normal" to be homosexual or bisexual. When Madonna and Britney Spears were photographed kissing each other, a forbidden boundary was removed. Now it is the rage among junior high and high school girls to take pictures of themselves kissing each other and post them on their MySpace.com pages. Anything goes.

Loss of community

God created people to live in families and to be part of His family. He created us for meaning and purpose through relationships. When we lose our families or our social moorings, loneliness, isolation, meaninglessness, and depression engulf us.

What we find in our communities today is that people are isolated from each other. Increased urbanization, broken families, and the loss of the sense of community all contribute to increased crime and gang activity. Cities such as Atlanta, Detroit, and Houston share the horrific distinction of being among those with the highest annual murder rate. Even Philadelphia—the "city of brotherly love"—has lost its redemptive identity as it has become an increasingly violent city.[5]

People don't always know why they are distressed. Many times people search for meaningful relationships in all the wrong places, or they make "relationships" into a god of sorts. Even in families that are intact, both parents are working outside the home. As a result, people can no longer depend on their families to be a refuge and a place where meaningful relationships produce healthy nurture, mentoring, and love.

Sometimes it seems like we're in the middle of an epidemic of depression. True warriors of God can combat the Goliath of social isolation by promoting the connectedness of the body of Christ.

On a CCN Webcast, Erwin McManus told the story of a man who had been part of their church, which is called Mosaic, for two or three years. He especially loved the small groups because of the relationships. Although he had never accepted Jesus Christ as his personal Savior during the time he had been at Mosaic, he told the pastor that he wanted to experience water baptism.

Why? Because he felt that, since he hadn't yet been baptized, he didn't fully belong. To him, *belonging* was the key. Although he was seeking baptism for the wrong reason, it underlines the cry for belonging.

This man represents an incredible harvest of lonely people who are unconnected, isolated, and lonely. These are the ones to whom the church can present the good news. They are saying, "Someone, notice me," and they are trying to find a way out of their despair.

Culture of death

Violent crime is only one aspect of an overall culture of death that is overtaking the nation. Through the legalization of abortion, we have become desensitized to death on a massive scale. Loneliness and depression create personal pain that is intense enough to lead to suicide.

A report cited by the *New York Times* stated: "With the homicide rate down sharply since the early 1990s, the number of Americans who commit suicide with guns each year now far surpasses those who are killed by others with firearms, government statistics show."[6] Yes, suicides take more lives in America than do homicides.

Among teenagers, most reports cite suicide as the third most common cause of death following accidental death first, and homicide second.[7] Something dark is happening among our teens.

Between 2003 and 2004, the largest increase ever in teen suicides occurred. *Science Daily* highlighted the statistics: "Following a decline of more than 28 percent, the suicide rate for 10- to 24-year-olds increased by 8 percent, the largest single-year rise in 15 years, according to a report just released in the Centers for Disease Control and Prevention's (CDC) *Morbidity and Mortality Weekly Report* (MMWR)."[8]

Some young people experiment with getting a high by hanging themselves. They unintentionally end up killing themselves trying to experience a euphoric state while diminishing the oxygen to the brain.[9] "Cutting" has also become commonplace. And anorexic young women are starving themselves to death.

Kids are accustomed to violence in their schools and in their gaming, while no thought is given to watching bloodshed in movies and on television. It is no longer particularly shocking to hear of yet another school shooting in which students or teachers have been murdered.

Have you ever heard of a toxic city? We have them here in the United States. Some cities are more toxic to live in than others because their sense of community has been eroded so badly. In 2004, Las Vegas had the highest divorce and suicide rate in the nation. Tacoma, Washington, was rated as the most stressful city to live in, followed by Miami, New Orleans, Las Vegas, and New York City. What made Tacoma so stressful? A high unemployment rate, high divorce rate, high suicide rate, constant cloudy weather, and a high rate of property crime.[10]

The aging of the population creates a new set of problems. For example, the highest suicide rate in the country is among white men over the age of sixty-five.[11]

Loss of freedoms

As much as we take our freedoms for granted in America, they are eroding. Significant freedoms have been forfeited in areas that I have already mentioned, such as the freedom to make decisions for ourselves and our children regarding sexual standards, birth control, and standards of discipline and behavior. In most states, parents have lost their right to give or withhold permission for their daughters to have an abortion. Health-care workers are being sued for holding to their Christian convictions when they conflict with those of the patient or the authorities. These are only a few examples.

We are still free to work, own a home, and have a family. Some of us, however, cannot take our Bibles to work. It is taboo to teach about Christianity in schools. But we can teach about Islam, Wicca, and much more, all in the name of tolerance and pluralism. We are no longer surprised when our child's swim meet gets scheduled for a Sunday morning, or when a Muslim airline passenger is allowed to put down his rug in the middle of the aisle to worship Allah at his designated prayer time.

GLOBAL THREATS

As if all these cultural trends are not bad enough, we must also contend with threats on a global scale. As a nation, as a church, and as individuals, our welfare and freedom are at stake.

Terrorism and Islam

Most experts believe that we have only begun to enter into an era of ongoing worldwide terrorism. From 9/11 on, Americans have learned to live under the shadow of terrorist threats.

Unrest in the Middle East and the influence of Islamic radicals set up disasters waiting to happen. Combine the oil shortage, Islamic fundamentalism, and anti-Semitism (with the goal of the destruction of Christians and Israel), and we have a time bomb ticking away in our front yard. A greater threat of terrorism arises out of the disenfranchised and economically disadvantaged young Muslim males in Europe and the Middle East than from the Muslim population of the United States, where potential violence is diffused by the higher standard of living, education, and opportunities.

Israel and the United States, which is called the Great Satan, are Islam's enemies. Joel Rosenberg, author of the book *Epicenter*, analyzes the Middle East conflict with Israel. He believes that we are currently living out Ezekiel 36–39. In other words, we have entered the end of the end.[12]

Do we who are the church understand where we are in history?

If we do, we will know that it's time to become warriors. We are faced not only with the Goliath of Islamofascism but also with the religious-spirit-driven force of homegrown terrorism, some of which arises out of misdirected churches. The religious spirit takes a public face when church members picket the funerals of homosexual servicemen who have died in the war in Iraq or when racial violence is commended in the name of God.

That's *not* the kinds of warriors I'm talking about. Such acts only serve to create more animosity toward the church, and they fail to extend the grace of God to sinners.

Demography

The philosopher Auguste Comte made the insightful statement, "Demography is destiny." He put his finger on a global threat to which warriors in the kingdom of God would do well to pay heed.

An interesting fact about the global situation is that population growth rates influence political decisions, economics, and military undertakings. This is especially true because of the population of young males who are naturally competitive, aggressive, territorial, and even violent in certain circumstances.

This observation was first put forward by Lionel Tiger and Robin Fox in their 1971 book, *The Imperial Animal*, where they posed the central question of any society or social system: "What do we do with the young males?"[13] Young males' aggression and competitiveness are fueled by their peak levels of testosterone, which is normal for their ages. Throughout history, societies have struggled with the challenge of controlling their young males' intense energy and channeling it into actions that benefit the society rather than damaging or destroying it. Some nations may even have gone to war, or considered going to war, for the primary purpose of channeling the aggression of their young male population. Both China and India must recognize this challenge before negative consequences override the positive ones.[14]

Along these lines, consider the following 2002 statistics:[15]

- In Muslim countries, 54 to 61.5 percent of the population is under the age of twenty-five.

- The disproportionate number of young Islamic males have mothers who encourage them to give their lives in war for the sake of Allah.

- In Pakistan, Saudi Arabia, and Afghanistan, the fertility rates are between 5.5 and 6.9 per woman. (The fertility rate essential to replace the existing population is 2.1.) These countries have rapidly growing populations, and they will continue to have a high percentage of young people.

- The United States can expect a population increase, but only because of the large Latino population, whose fertility rate is 3.0. Some prognosticators say that the U.S. will eventually become part of the Southern Hemisphere demographically because of the burgeoning Latino population.

In summary, changing cultural trends in every sector of American society are creating a world that is foreign to us. In many cases we have not adequately recognized this fact, nor do we know what to do with it. These trends are not only unique to the United States, but they are also global, threatening nationalistic thinking, and demanding creative, God-given solutions. To deal with these Goliaths, we need to seek wisdom from God.

Economic shifts

We are riding the edge of fiscal disaster in the United States. Since the Great Depression, our economy has never been more fragile. Even the value of our dollar is at an all-time low.

Whether we recognize it or not, our nation is no longer the privileged world financial leader. Worldwide, a new middle class is arising. China, India, the oil-producing nations, and other nations now "own" us through the globalization of outsourcing and investment. It is estimated by different thinkers that by the years 2025 to 2040, China will be the economic leader of the world.[16]

OTHER DAUNTING CHALLENGES

The issues I just related to you do not exhaust the list of daunting trends and threats that are now coming to the forefront. Here are two more challenges, each of which can loom large as a Goliath:

Political crises

Politics and power go together. A political crisis is a power crisis, a leadership crisis. As we know, the political world has come to be dominated more by a competition for power rather than righteous servant leadership of a church, city, state, or nation. We desperately need leaders who will not get into power wars, but who will exercise their authority for the purpose of positioning people to fulfill their destiny for their prosperity and posterity.

David had a God-centered view of power. It was given to him for the sake of the people—for their good. The Bible says, "David realized that the Lord had established him as king over Israel, and that his kingdom was highly exalted, for the sake of His people Israel" (1 Chron. 14:2, NAS).

Gender crisis

God took woman out of the side of man so that they could lead together. The apostolic commissioning of Genesis 1:28 was given to both male and female. How can God's harvest take place without a reconciliation of male and female? Just as a physical baby cannot be conceived without both a man and a woman, so it is in the spiritual.

We see women taking their places in the marketplace, but the church is lagging behind in this regard. More women are being educated in American universities than men, and they will be increasingly assuming places of leadership. "For the 2001–2002 academic year, enrollment in U.S. colleges was 54 percent female."[17]

Some of us are called specifically to fight Goliaths of global proportions, including massive economic problems, disruptive social imbalances, terrorist threats, and national crises. But please bear in mind that no one person can take on any of these giants single-handedly. These global enemies are like immense Philistine armies, employing shifting tactics and making new alliances as they take territory. Such armies will only yield to another army—a disciplined army of God's warriors in which each warrior handles one assignment at a time.

In your own combat with economic issues, for instance, you may find yourself doing something as simple and hidden as getting your personal finances in order and being generous with your money. If that is your assignment, do it faithfully.

Just because you aren't in a position of authority on the front lines doesn't mean you aren't a warrior who has a part to play. Your very lifestyle is a form of warfare. Remember Paul's assurance in Romans 16:19–20: "I want you to be wise in what is good and innocent in what is evil. The God of peace will soon crush Satan under your feet" (NAS).

HAVE WE LOST OUR HEART FOR WAR?

When Russia invaded Afghanistan, it is said that, because of the outcry of mothers, Russia had to pull its troops out and suffered a defeat as a result. The mothers could not bear the loss of their sons. Not so in Islamic nations where it is an honor to be the mother of a son who has died for Allah. To them, martyrdom is a virtue.[18]

Furthermore, in those impoverished, second- and third-world nations, growing numbers of well-educated, disenchanted young people have no place to work. These young people are overeducated for their culture and have developed middle-class tastes. Their frustration and disillusionment feed cultural and political conflict.[19] They are both willing and eager to fight.

Are we equipped to face such odds? Could it be that America has lost its heart to fight wars?

In the United States (at least prior to the war in Iraq), members of the armed forces joined up primarily to obtain an education. No longer did most men and women join the armed forces to defend the future of their nation, to protect their fathers and mothers, sons and daughters. They joined for personal gain. They joined the National Guard and became "weekend warriors."

Part of our challenge with the situation in Iraq right now is the fact that many of our forces who have been sent there are reservists. They have been adequately trained, but it was on weekends. That's what most of them signed up for—weekends only. Consequently, they are going into battle, but they never intended to be full-time *members of the armed forces.*

I believe the church has been somewhat like our armed forces; we've been weekend warriors too. We have not taken on the warrior role as a lifestyle. I am not only talking about the generation of young adults; I'm also talking about a church generation. An entire generation of the church must arise as warriors if we are going to turn the culture of this nation and protect it from ungodly threats.

To do this, we can't be only occasional warriors. If we are supposed to be part of the army of transformation for our nation and the world, we must become daily warriors—people who wake up in the morning as warriors, people who don't take a vacation from the warrior mentality.

We need to be prepared. We need to undertake a program of tough training and discipline. This means something is going to have to shift in our worldview because most of us became believers with the assumption that our lives would be of the "happily ever after" variety and now we would be home free.

Actually, the war starts when we become believers. As new believers, we begin a program of training and discipline that can turn us from civilians into soldiers. It's not a weekend-only training, as you may have noticed in your own experience. Day in and day out we are under the command of the Most High God, the Lion of the tribe of Judah, the Captain of the hosts.

EQUIPPED AND PREPARED

To find out more about what the military mind-set is like, I asked Jennifer Waddell, a member of the church I pastor and a former enlisted military officer, to write something about her experience. Her reflections on the military mind-set open up the subject in a new way:

> When I first joined the military, I had anything but a military mind-set. I was focused on me, myself, and I. Little did I know

that over the next ten-plus years, God was going to give me a military mind-set.

When I joined the air force, I had to learn how to put myself lower and farther down on the priority list of life. The idea that there really are things more important than my comfort and what I want was a totally new concept for me—to believe that there was a cause greater than my financial security and my future.

I had to learn to follow orders. That was the biggest hurdle. I didn't want anyone telling me what to do, when to do it, or how to do it. I remember telling my mother when I was about sixteen that I didn't mind doing things around the house such as cleaning, doing dishes, cooking, and the like. I just didn't like being told to do it. Being under authority was a part of the military mind-set that I did not come in with. It took me a long time to learn it.

What does it mean to have a military mind-set? Someone with a military mind-set understands authority, loyalty, and commitment. A militarily minded person understands war, discipline, order, and the importance of obedience. The person respects and honors those in authority. If you have a military mind-set, you love not your life, even unto death. You are willing to lay down your life for a cause greater than yourself.

When I joined the military, I had to be taught all of these things. At first, they were no more a part of me than the clothes I wore. I could put my clothes on; I could take them off. I could change them at will. But one day I put them on and I didn't take them off anymore because they had become a part of me. So even when there was no one standing in front of me barking orders, I found myself automatically and naturally following those orders. I was disciplined, orderly, and obedient. I was a woman under authority.

It took me awhile to get there. During my second year of military service, I was scheduled to go to small arms training. I was deathly afraid of guns. Count me out. I just did not show up for the appointment.

Wrong move! I found out that there were consequences to disobedience.

I was given a warning, rescheduled for the next class, and threatened with an Article 15 if I missed the next class. For those of you who don't know, an Article 15 is a form of discipline authorized by Article 15 of the Uniform Code of Military Justice. Commanders are permitted to administratively discipline troops without a court-martial, and this disciplinary action is placed in their service record. An Article 15 is not a good thing to have on your record.

I did go to the next class, even with all my fears. God did not deliver me from it, but He gave me mega-grace in the midst of it. I did very well too, achieving an expert rating. We were allowed to keep our practice targets and take them home with us if we wanted to. So I kept mine for a while to show off all my bull's-eyes. I had hit the mark almost every time. That showed divine intervention as far as I was concerned.

Obedience really is better than sacrifice, and it is a part of the military mind-set. Being obedient is important not only for our own welfare but also for the sake of those who are fighting alongside us. If this had been a war situation instead of small arms training, physical training, staff meetings, or other training circumstance, someone's life might have been put in danger because I was not in my place.

Of all the aspects of a military mind-set, I believe that the three most important things are *authority, loyalty,* and *commitment.* I had to learn that it was not all about me, but it was about a nation of people who were depending on me and others for their safety and protection. We all played a very important role in the support and defense of our nation. It was not about who wore the stars and the bars, or the stripes, but about all of us, in whatever position we were in, doing our part to protect and defend our nation.

We can really accomplish something when we can each stand in the places that we have been assigned without jealousy or envy, doing the tasks that we have been called to do with all of our hearts. That's a tall order, but that is what a military mind-set is all about.

Having a military mind-set also means that I understand war. There is a real enemy out there who does not have my best interests at heart. But how do I fight this enemy?

A military mind-set understands that you cannot fight by yourself. In order to win the battle, you have to work together with a team of people who are different from you and who have different abilities and resources. Before I can even think of going to battle with this team of people, I need to know that they will watch my back, so to speak, and they need to know that they can depend on me as well.

The military knows and understands the importance of a team. They make you eat together, sleep together, work together, live together, and so on, so that you will have the same mind-set and the same heart.

My family and I lived in base housing while I was on active duty. My co-workers were not merely co-workers; they were also my neighbors. We worshiped together, went shopping together, went to the same movie theater, went bowling together. After a few years of doing everything together, you tend to become family. It's not hard to lay down your life for your family. Sometimes family members don't get along, but let someone from the outside mess with any of them, and you will see the family pull together against the opposition.

One more thing about the military mind-set: when I raised my right hand to be commissioned as an officer of the U.S. Air Force, I was not necessarily signing up to go to war and die. That was not on my list of things to do while I was in the military. But I knew that any time I was in a war situation, there would be the possibility that I might have to make the ultimate sacrifice.

Jesus willingly laid down His life for real; it was His authentic choice. He was willing to obey the Father, to submit to the Father's will, so that we could live. Jesus loved not His life even unto death. Most of all, having a military mind-set means that I am becoming more like Him.

Getting Our Heart Back

How do we ordinary believers get a military mind-set? How do we become equipped and prepared for war? The Captain of the hosts trains us by sending us into skirmishes. That's how David became toughened in mind, spirit, and body as he tended his father's sheep and he took on the lion and the bear that attacked them.

As we undergo training, we begin to change from people who are influenced by the culture around us to people who are capable of changing the culture. Our training causes us to grow in our character, and it enlarges our grasp of God's truth. We find our place in the big picture, and we learn to be responsive and obedient to the orders of our Commander in Chief.

If we are to transform this nation, we have to become daily warriors who wake up every morning, seven days a week, with a warrior mentality. With a full awareness of the risks involved, we learn to make sure that everything we do is in the will of God. The minute we're outside His will (doing the convenient or comfortable thing or taking matters into our own hands), we get out from under the protection of God.

I don't want to frighten you, but it's true. Disobeying God or making a decision for the wrong reason puts us at the mercy of the enemy.

I hope you realize that there is even a war over staying in the will of God. In my own state of Michigan, there are believers who are leaving the state—the place God had assigned them to be—solely because of economic conditions.

Did God tell them to move to a more prosperous state? Not all of them. That's like a soldier deciding that he just doesn't care for the lack of comforts that come with his military life, so he goes AWOL—and then wonders why he gets in trouble for it. They may end up more prosperous, but they will starve spiritually, finding that passion, zeal, and the very life of God have been depleted from their heart.

A word used for a company of soldiers is *troops*. Think about that word! Warriors are troopers. They just get back up and keep on going. They don't give up, nor do they give in. They keep going when they're tired and hungry, even when they don't really know where they're headed.

Warriors are guardsmen. The word *shamar* in Hebrew means "to guard." Part of your warrior anointing means you will guard what has been entrusted to you. You start with your personal inheritance—your right standing with God, your own family. It's the *shamar* anointing in action.

Warriors are also guerillas. I love this because guerillas don't fight wars in a normal way. They fight using unconventional means or maneuvers. They know how to scatter the enemy. Part of the church's guerilla warfare involves diffusing the enemy's strength by coming in the opposite spirit. When you come in with love, you can disarm hate. You don't always need guns and swords; sometimes all you need is a godly and wise word or two.

Most of us, when confronted with anger, respond in a spirit of anger ourselves. Instead we should turn to our ever-present Guide for marching orders.

Sometimes you may feel that most of your life is devoted to what seems like "little stuff"—training, skirmishes, persevering, helping others get back up. But if you have ever been a soldier, you will realize that most of your job description is little stuff like that. What it adds up to is readiness for war. It adds up to a restoration of the warrior mentality and a heart for combat.

Not all warfare is pulling down a high place on Mount Kilimanjaro. For most of us, it is facing day-to-day conflicts and minor hostilities with the people around us. That is our training, and that is our war.

FOOT SOLDIERS

Even as warriors, most people are like foot soldiers in World War II, enlisted men who seldom felt like heroes. We're ordinary people, by and large; we are not going to become famous—or infamous. Each has some small role to play. Sometimes we may feel more like a cog in the wheel, if that. But every one of us counts.

Philip Yancey captures this well:

Faith also gets tested when a sense of God's presence fades or when the very ordinariness of life makes us question whether our responses even matter. We wonder, "What can one person do? What difference will my small effort make?"

I once watched a public television series based on interviews with survivors from World War II. The soldiers recalled how they spent a particular day. One sat in the foxhole all day; once or twice, a German tank drove by, and he shot at it. Others played cards and frittered away the time. A few got involved in furious firefights. Mostly, the day passed like any other day for an infantryman on the front. Later, they learned they had just participated in one of the largest, most decisive engagements of the war, the Battle of the Bulge. It did not *feel* decisive to any of them at the time, because none had the big picture of what was happening elsewhere.

Great victories are won when ordinary people execute their assigned tasks—and a faithful person does not debate each day whether he or she is in the mood to follow the sergeant's orders or show up at a boring job. We exercise faith by responding to the task that lies before us, for we have control only over our actions in the present moment.[20]

HEARING THE CALL

What I have been trying to say is that each one of us needs to step up to the challenges (the Goliaths, if you will) that have stormed the world we live in.

Today in the United States, we live in a very different world from the one we started out in. If you and I fail to apprehend this, we will do one of two things: we will identify the wrong issues and therefore fight the wrong war, or we will fail to fight at all. That is, assuming that all of these varied issues will flush themselves out over time and everything will be all right.

So what do you and I need in this hour? We need wisdom and understanding and knowledge so that we can become Davidic warriors. We need courage to advance in spite of fear and vulnerability. We need to be very clear in our minds and hearts as to whom we serve and how we serve Him—every single minute, twenty-four hours a day, seven days a week, like a soldier in the military.

Are you there yet?

4

Goliath Demands a David

As I stood on Israel's Mount of Olives back in 2006, I came to the realization that we, the church, are facing an enemy that is like a Goliath. It seemed more real to me than the time of the huge 9/11 assault on our nation in 2001.

I looked down over Jerusalem, and I wept. Perhaps in a small way I was touching what Jesus touched when He looked down over the city and said, "O Jerusalem, Jerusalem...How often I wanted to gather your children together, as a hen gathers her chicks under her wings, but you were not willing!" (Matt. 23:37).

I was in travail. I doubt that I felt the grief as deeply as Jesus did, because I'm so cluttered with the stuff of this world in my mind and heart. Yet clearly my heart was breaking. I was in travail for Israel and for the United States. At that moment I felt as if I would risk my own life for a cause that transcended the small world in which I live.

I could not see any answers. I did not glimpse any light slipping through cracks in a window shade. All I could see was darkness, pain, and the potential for great destruction. Standing in the midst of a very fragile peace between warring forces, it felt as if the whole world could blow up at any moment.

Yet there in the midst of this unseen war and conflict, I had tapped into the heart of God. His heart was broken over this situation too.

A Goliath, a Snake

I surveyed the magnitude of the issue. I saw an anti-Semitic Goliath who, like a snake, has coiled itself around the world. He is like a python, seeking to squeeze the life out of the world as we know it, to kill it.

That snake has wrapped itself around Israel and is bent on destroying that nation as well as all covenant people, which includes Christians like you and me. It has wrapped itself around other nations too, capturing them in an irrational grip of greed and hatred.

Oil is part of its lifeblood because oil controls the wealth of the world. Nations bow at the feet of this Goliath, this snake, simply to obtain a substance that will sustain their economies. (You know what I'm talking about. Because they possess the world's richest oil fields, the Middle Eastern Islamic nations possess the trump card at this time in history.) More than this, religion has formed an irrational base of support for hatred. Religious hatred of all that Jews and Christians stand for has provided fuel for the conflict.

Held in Its Grip

Going back into the city of Jerusalem again, I entered a restaurant across the street from where the infamous bus 32A had been blown up by a suicide bomber. As I sat there with several people, two of whom pastor a church in Jerusalem, the wife told me how she and her child just missed getting on that bus by a mere five minutes.

Another woman in the group, who is also a Jewish leader, described the continuing danger to which Israelis have grown accustomed. Far from being an occasional passing mishap, it is their daily reality. They are constantly on edge. Proportionately, far more Israeli citizens have died from suicide bombings than American citizens did from 9/11.

Later I made the short trip to Bethlehem, which is so close to Jerusalem that it is like a suburb. Bethlehem, the place where Jesus was born, has become such a dangerous place that a high wall has been built between the two cities in an attempt to reduce the suicide bombings. (Islamic citizens of Bethlehem have come into Jerusalem as suicide bombers.) It took me five minutes to enter Bethlehem and forty-five minutes to get back into Jerusalem. The security screening was slow because it was so laborious and thorough. I was told that the wall has, in fact, significantly reduced the number of bombing incidents.

Bethlehem is now the home of Arabs, both Christian and Muslim. I walked the streets, aware of the constant danger, processing my own feelings of internal conflict. On the one hand I had compassion for the people because of the danger they live with continually. I was overcome, depressed, disillusioned, and in some way tortured by the fact of the invisible but very real environment of danger that is their daily experience. I also felt almost guilty because of the comparative ease and comfort of my life back home in the States.

CAPTURED BY GOLIATH

Now I had to deal with my own hatred; I found myself feeling disdain for the Muslims. This was hatred for a people group, and it did not represent the heart of God. I felt that they were like mad animals who live and act out of an irrational hatred. I felt that this hatred had started because of the war between Isaac and Ishmael and had been perpetuated and escalated because of the conflict between Jacob and Esau. But I was unable to see past it.

I started by reminding myself that it was Abraham and Sarah, who are members of "faith's hall of fame" (in Hebrews 11), who initially created the problem. Since I am a descendent of Abraham, I stand as responsible as they did.

God loved the world so much—not just the church, but the whole world—that He gave His only Son to die for them. (See John 3:16.) At that point I had to repent, but I was not even close to being willing to die for the Muslims, or even to sacrifice something on their behalf. I had just rejected a part of the world that Christ had died for, the Muslim world. I had narrowed the word *world* in John 3:16 down to Jews and Christians.

In other words, I had just been hooked by the spirit behind the whole problem; something had caused me to want to hate. This was something big, and it was hidden. It was concealed, invisible to the ordinary eye. It was an unseen spirit that fueled something ugly, not only between individuals but also between people groups and between nations. It was a true Goliath.

GOD ENTERS THE FIELD

That day in Jerusalem, I remembered something I had read in a book called *Great Revivals* by Colin C. Whitaker. This book had captured my attention in a pile of marked-down books at a Christian bookstore. (I am a voracious reader, always looking for a good new book to read.) In it the author quoted something that Dr. Martyn Lloyd-Jones had written in his book *Preaching and Preachers:*

> I know of nothing, in my own experience, that has been more exhilarating and helpful, and that acted more frequently as a tonic to me, than the history of revivals....Church history, and especially the history of revivals, is one of the best antidotes to a believer's discouragement and depression in the time we are living in.[1]

Whitaker then went on to say, "Revival has been described as the fourth R, the three Rs being reformation (doctrine), renewal (dynamics), and restoration (direction); but revival is God taking the field."[2]

I had been attracted to this book because, as a product of revival myself, I have always been captured by the thought of revival and awakening. I love to read about revivals, listen to stories about revival, and talk to people who have lived through revival. I hunger for and pray for revival, the supernatural reality of God fully manifest on Earth, reviving His church and then awakening unbelievers to the reality of Christ, removing the veil of deception from their mind.

In some ways I have felt like a carrier of revival—revival for believers and conversion for unbelievers. This thought captured my attention: "Revival is God taking the field."

I saw Goliath, standing in the middle of the field, taunting the puny army of Israel. I saw David, stepping forth on the field to take him on. In the person of David, God was taking the field!

Are you and I not dealing with "fields" now? Could we not equate this to kingdoms?

My mind raced over all the fields that I currently stand in or that I am aware of, fields that exist in my world, in my state, in my nation. All those fields are up for grabs. Something or someone wants them. Some have already fallen into the hands of a Goliath. Yet they don't have to remain in his hands—when God enters the field.

THE KING AND I: TAKING THE FIELD

Is revival really the end goal or is it the *field* that God is after? I propose that the fields are the arenas, areas, or spheres that are ruled by something or someone. They are kingdoms, if you will. Many of them already have Goliaths standing in the middle of them.

In this day, God is facing down Goliaths. And He does it by sending Davids—you and me—into the fields.

God came to Earth as a man—Jesus—and, to this day, His Spirit does His work through people. Jesus came as a man to demonstrate that through the power of His Father, every challenge could be overcome. Therefore we, as human beings, have a model of a man who overcame. He has chosen people to be His colaborers and coheirs. (See Romans 8:16–17; 1 Corinthians 3:9.)

So King Jesus comes through you and me. He comes to face Goliath in the middle of the field.

You and I have been chosen to rule and reign with Christ. We are to stand in the field with Him and release His authority, ruling over that particular field. We are to take our place with God as our source, and we are to position ourselves in authority over the field that God has given us.

Prior to this, you and I may have had a long season of testing, of being tried. Our connectedness to God and our endurance in the face of trouble has now prepared us to rule and reign with Christ in this new season. Now we are qualified to become victorious warriors:

> If we endure, *we shall also reign with Him.*
> —2 TIMOTHY 2:12, EMPHASIS ADDED

> You were slain, and have redeemed us to God by Your blood out of every tribe and tongue and people and nation, and have made us kings and priests to our God; and *we shall reign on the earth.*
> —REVELATION 5:9–10, EMPHASIS ADDED

WHAT IS YOUR GOLIATH?

So you see, there are many Goliaths standing in different fields today. These are giants who are attempting to rule what is supposed to belong to God. Fields represent many things—aspects of government, the church, education, business, the family and society, media and the arts, and so forth. In some sectors of Christianity, it is being referred to as the "7 Mountains,"[3] referring to a common, historical revelation that Bill Bright and Loren Cunningham originally shared and then communicated to us as believers.

The basic mandate of Goliath, as we see it portrayed in 1 Samuel 17, is to take over that which belongs to God and His people. This power seeks to rule for purposes other than God's purposes. The source of Goliath's power is not God; it is an evil power. A Goliath is a giant who represents a very powerful and intimidating demonic structure. He stands against God and His covenant people, and he tries to take their territory.

Goliath stands in the middle of our future. He stands in the middle of powerful trends in the world that have the potential to create great breakthrough, wealth, communication, and more; they also have the potential, however, for great destruction. It's as if we are living in the best of times and the worst of times. It's not an either/or situation but rather a both/and one. We live with energy shortages and climate changes. We live with economic transformation wrought by globalization. And we live with the "war on terror," which has barely begun.

As the church (this means you and me), we have many Goliaths standing up in many fields to destroy us. At the start of this chapter, I described the Goliath in the Middle East that seeks to overtake and destroy Israel and any nation that aligns with Israel. What about the Goliath of abortion that continues to destroy a generation of potential warriors, a generation that has had its life, its voice, stolen from it? Is there not also an anarchic attitude that is subtly increasing in strength in our nation, which will at some point threaten the viability of our governmental system?

Think of other Goliaths: lawlessness, violence, greed, racism, anti-Semitism, religion, immorality. The list goes on and on. Sometimes it seems as if we are on the verge of extinction as a society. There are too many Goliaths.

GOLIATH DEMANDS A DAVID

The real issue is this: to what or to whom will I bow down and worship? Worship requires a master and a servant. Will I serve a Goliath or will I serve God? It's that simple.

I can't serve both of them, because they are archenemies. Jesus said, "No one can serve two masters; for either he will hate the one and love the other, or else he will be loyal to the one and despise the other" (Matt. 6:24). The ruler of heaven and Earth is the Lord Jesus Christ. The evil one and the enemy is Satan. They go head-to-head in battle. They are at war, and we are the warriors in God's army.

Those of us who belong to the living God know that we owe our very existence to Him. We are His offspring. "In Him we live and move and have our being" (Acts 17:28). We know that He created both the heavens and the earth. We know that without Him—Jesus, the Word—nothing was made that has been made. (See John 1:3.) He's the originator. We know that without Him, we can do nothing. (See John 15:5.) Consequently, when we arise to counter the enemy, we must rise up as people whose sole source is God, people who bow down and worship God alone as He is revealed through Jesus Christ.

Goliath *can* be conquered by people who have been created, called, and anointed by God. But Goliath demands a David. Only a David will be able to defeat a Goliath. And David was handpicked by the Lord.

What made David uniquely qualified? When Saul lost his anointing because of his disobedience, the prophet Samuel was directed by God to quit mourning for Saul. God instructed Samuel to get up, go find the new king, and anoint him. He didn't tell Samuel who that person would be.

God led Samuel to Jesse's sons, telling him to look at the heart of the man rather than his outer appearance.

> When they entered, he looked at Eliab and thought, "Surely the Lord's anointed is before Him." But the LORD said to Samuel, "Do not look at his appearance or at the height of his stature, because I have rejected him; for God sees not as man sees, for man looks at the outward appearance, but the LORD looks at the heart."
>
> —1 SAMUEL 16:6–7, NAS

Samuel had assumed that Eliab was the one—he must have looked like a king. Of course, David was very good-looking as well, a striking young man with beautiful eyes. But it wasn't about looks. To deal with both Goliath and Saul, the anointed one needed to have a pure heart. Someone who was entangled in the affairs of this life would not be able to defeat a Goliath. In the New Testament, we read, "No one engaged in warfare entangles himself with the affairs of this life, that he may please him who enlisted him as a soldier" (2 Tim. 2:4).

So Samuel went through the first seven sons of Jesse. When he had finished with the seventh son, he knew that none of them was the right one, so he asked Jesse if he had another son. David was called in, and the Lord told Samuel, "This is the one!" (1 Sam. 16:12).

David was the eighth son. One meaning of the number eight is "new beginnings." The number is also symbolic of infinity or eternity. It is a "forever."

With David, God was going to begin a new thing. To do so, He needed a man with a new heart, a new spirit. This man would enter the fields set before him and conquer them. He would rule in the new thing that God was doing.

Furthermore, God was saying that David was a shadow or a type of the king who would rule and reign forever. He was the archetype perpetuated through Jesus Christ and then in the life of every believer throughout history. That includes you and me.

> Then Samuel took the horn of oil and anointed David in the midst of his brothers; and the Spirit of the Lord came mightily upon David from that day forward.
>
> —1 SAMUEL 16:13, AMP

A DAVIDIC HEART

I believe that we are in a day when God is anointing men and women, not according to their outward qualifications or appearance, but according to their hearts. He needs pure-hearted men and women to rule and reign with Him, men and women who can defeat Goliaths. Their pure hearts are fixed fully on God.

They are not sinless—neither was David. Yet even in the midst of sin, they are, like David, fully transparent before God. When they sin, they don't fight or run; they immediately yield to God as David did. It's the difference between a religious mind-set and a truly spiritual one.

God's warriors look a lot like Jesus. Benjamin Deitrick is a young man who is the media and video director for Eagles' Wings Ministries in Clarence, New York, the ministry founded and directed by Robert Stearns. I asked Benjamin this question: What do you think it means to be a warrior? His reply was straightforward.

> I think of the chief warrior who has ever walked this earth, the One whose example we are to follow. Jesus was sent by His Father to the ultimate battleground where He would be tested severely, mistreated, and killed, and where He would receive His mantle as our warrior King.
>
> He was set apart in humility and consecration, completely obedient and submissive to the One who was giving Him orders. He was as bold and strong as a lion, and yet as innocent and gentle as a dove. He fought the battle not as the world fights, with arrogance and pride and physical strength, but with love and kindness and the authority that comes from a compassionate heart.
>
> We have been taught that the pathway to greatness includes exalting ourselves as well as tirelessly promoting the "kingdom of self." Will we see through this and respond to God's call? Or will we be just one more generation who misses their mandate and calling because we see nothing but the deceptive mask of self? We need to look to the true Commander in Chief of our army and lay down our lives for His Father's kingdom even as He did.

The other day I was reading Philip Yancey's book *Soul Survivor*, which is an account of Yancey's heroes and how they achieved that status in his life.[4] This is my second time reading it. I love the way

Yancey writes about the people he admires, many of whom are the same people I have admired.

One chapter tells about Martin Luther King Jr. As I read the account of King's life, I thought of David. King was not a perfect man. In fact, he had what some would consider very serious character flaws. (I consider them flaws also.) Yet he totally submitted to the will of God and became the leader of the civil rights movement.

This was his arena, his field. And there was racial segregation, one of the most daunting Goliaths of the twentieth century, standing in the middle of it. He took it on. Day after day he faced it, unrelentingly pursuing the Goliath of segregation until it bowed and surrendered. In the process, Martin Luther King Jr. was martyred for the cause.

Others must face personal Goliaths first. Crystal Harvey is a young woman who had to do that. Crystal is now a leader in our church as well as at her place of work in the secular field. She already has her BA degree from Eastern Michigan University. She is aspiring to become a writer and is planning toward a graduate degree to prepare her. Here is her story:

> When I was a senior in high school, I went through an emotional and psychological breakdown that threatened the very future of my life. I was being told by doctors that I might not be able to graduate with my class, that I might never be able to live a normal life again. In one night, I went from being a straight-A student to not being able to put a sentence together.
>
> Some of my family and friends were telling me that I had to cooperate with the doctors, while others were telling me that the doctors were making things worse and that I needed to just trust God for healing. As the battle intensified around me and

within me, I had no idea what to do or how to handle what I was going through. All I knew to do was pray, stand, and rely on God as the only One who could fully heal and restore me.

I think that warriors often have to march to the beat of a different drummer. They cannot listen to everyone and expect to win their battles. When David fought Goliath, he didn't have much support—even his brothers ridiculed his confidence against the Philistine giant. The very army that should have backed him shouted doubting words from behind as his enemy simultaneously cursed him to his face. What if David had listened to the voices of his enemy and his unbelieving kinfolk? What if Joshua and Caleb had decided to yield to the popular belief that they were mere grasshoppers compared to their enemy? What if I had given ear to the doctors who told me I might not have a future to look forward to?

Warriors can't allow the voices of doubt to keep them from running into battle. They don't allow the enemy to intimidate them out of their God-given promises. Warriors have a different spirit. It's not that they don't see and experience the giants or the obstacles. They see them, but they understand that He who is in them is greater. They barge right through those obstacles and defeat the enemy.

After a grueling month and a half, God did heal me. He did restore me. I *was* able to graduate with my class and to go on to college fully healed. The Lord became my personal healer.

LOVE AND MILITANCY

You and I are called to fight for Christ's honor and to do it the way David did. He was both a lover and a warrior. Even the name *David* means "to boil hot."[5] David was passionate. Everything he did, he did with passion because he loved deeply. In the same way, you and I are called to a passion that arises out of an intense love.

David abandoned himself to the will of God. He was raised up to deliver Israel from its last enemies. He faced the possibility of losing his life. But David's heart was so knit to God's that he was willing to give up his life for the cause of God, to love not his life unto death. (See Revelation 12:11.)

Out of love, David was called to contend with Goliath. When we contend with our Goliaths, we do it in the same way—God's way. "To contend" means "to strive with determination or exertion in a rivalry or contest, striving against all difficulties, exigencies, or failings."

To contend also means that we argue for what we believe to be right. We maintain the truth. We struggle to vanquish our opponents and to overcome difficulties and adversity because of something we hold dear.

What do I hold dear? The Lord my God. I love Him with my whole heart, mind, and strength. Therefore I will contend on His behalf for what is right.

ANOINTED TO DESTROY GOLIATH AND TO RULE

From the day that Samuel took the horn of oil and anointed David as king in the sight of his brothers, God's Spirit came mightily upon David. Instead of being the "tail," the little brother who kept track of the sheep, David subdued the last enemies of Israel.

He was no longer what he had been in the past. He had become the head! He was now a king, a warrior, a ruler. He had been anointed for his new identity, to rule and reign in the power of God.

David was qualified to overcome Goliath through that act of commissioning. He now had a legal right to go out into battle and to fight for the sake of God's kingdom. This one act gave him the "knowing" as well as the authority he needed.

Just like David, you and I have been anointed. We received power when we were baptized in the Holy Spirit. "You shall receive power when the Holy Spirit has come upon you; and you shall be witnesses to Me in Jerusalem, and in all Judea and Samaria, and to the end of the earth" (Acts 1:8).

Furthermore, we became witnesses. In the Greek, the word *witness* means both "record" and "martyr." Through the character and power of God working through us, we are to be a living, breathing, walking record of God. Paul said that the people were the epistles that men read, convincing them of the validity of his ministry. (See 2 Corinthians 3:1–2.) That means us. You and I are the epistles, the records that people read. We are walking, talking records of the power and presence of God to the world.

We are also martyrs. That doesn't mean that all of us are going to die a martyr's death before we reach the end of our natural life span. The word *martyr* does mean to die for a cause, but it can mean that we sacrifice our lives on behalf of a cause. We give up the right to ourselves. We surrender our wishes and our desires to God.

Could this be what it means to say that if a grain of wheat falls into the ground and dies, it will not remain alone but will bear much fruit? (See John 12:24.) Could it be that if we surrender ourselves fully to God's purposes, we will become far more fruitful than if we had held on to our limited view of ourselves?

Think again about David. He gave himself away to God. The day he was anointed with oil was the last day that he had a right to do what he wanted when he wanted to do it. Yet it was that day that he became qualified to kill Goliath. It was that day that David came into his destiny. This is what he had been born for.

I have been tapped on the shoulder by the holy God, through His Holy Spirit, and I have been filled with both miraculous power and the ability to arise and accomplish something that otherwise would not be possible. I have been chosen and anointed to be a giant-killer. I have been born for this. So have you, and so has the church.

Will you arise and go into the field God has delivered into your hands? Will you slay the Goliath who stands in the middle of it, threatening you? This is the crucial moment, the turning point for us as the church and as a nation. If we do not arise in response to the Lord's clear call, we will remain in a wilderness of wandering as the Israelites did.

Goliath is standing on your land and mine. He is taunting us. We need to go out there and defeat him. Our Goliath demands a David. You and I are of the eighth son who became the firstborn, Jesus Christ, the One who initiated the new beginning, the One who sits on the throne of David forever.

> The LORD said to my Lord, "Sit at My right hand, till I make
> Your enemies Your footstool." The LORD shall send the rod of
> Your strength out of Zion. Rule in the midst of Your enemies!
> —PSALM 110:1–2

We have been chosen to rule and to reign with Him forever. Let's start doing it now, ruling in the midst of our enemies.

5

One Small Stone

THE DAY THAT DAVID FACED GOLIATH WAS AN ordinary day. It was probably uncomfortably hot, Israel was at war, and David was the kid brother who had stayed at home tending the sheep.

Oh, sure, David had been anointed king the day before when Samuel poured oil all over him, ruining his shepherd's outfit. Yes, amazingly, the Spirit of God had come all over him from that day forward. But he was still David, the youngest of eight children. How did this ordinary young guy end up out on this battlefield facing Goliath, this big, foul-mouthed monstrosity of a warrior weighted down with armor?

David's father had asked him to take food to his three older brothers Eliab, Abinadab, and Shammah, who were part of Saul's army, and also to their captain (1 Sam. 17:13). Jesse didn't say, "Go out onto the battlefield and become a hero." He just dispatched David with the lunch buckets:

> Then Jesse said to his son David, "Take now for your brothers an ephah of this dried grain and these ten loaves, and run to your brothers at the camp. And carry these ten cheeses to the captain of their thousand, and see how your brothers fare, and bring back news of them."
>
> —1 SAMUEL 17:17–18

It was the lunch. A simple lunch delivery positioned David before Goliath. It can be the same with us. Some ordinary assignment can land us in the middle of a life-and-death, Goliath situation.

After David arrived at the camp with the food, he got up to speed in a hurry regarding what was going on. He left the lunches with the supply keeper and ran to see the army. Right then Goliath came out to taunt the army of Israel, as he had done the day before:

> While they were talking together, the Philistine champion, Goliath of Gath, stepped out from the front lines of the Philistines, and gave his usual challenge. David heard him.
>
> —1 SAMUEL 17:23, THE MESSAGE

What was Goliath's "usual challenge"? Here's how *The Message* depicts his challenge from the previous days:

> Goliath stood there and called out to the Israelite troops, "Why bother using your whole army? Am I not Philistine enough for you? And you're all committed to Saul, aren't you? So pick your best fighter and pit him against me. If he gets the upper hand and kills me, the Philistines will all become your slaves. But if I get the upper hand and kill him, you'll all become our slaves and serve us. I challenge the troops of Israel this day. Give me a man. Let us fight it out together!"
>
> —1 SAMUEL 17:8–10, THE MESSAGE

Is this not representative of the daunting challenges that you and I are up against? Are not the Goliaths of today taunting us, daring us to stand up and defeat them? They are overconfident; they consider themselves undefeatable. But as far as the Davidic generation is concerned, their taunts are a clarion call to engage in the battle at hand. We can learn how to respond from David's story.

FACE-OFF

An insignificant assignment had brought David face-to-face with his destiny. Maybe his audacity came from the fact that he was young. Perhaps it came from his anointing by Samuel. I have a hunch that it was the latter reason because 1 Samuel 16:13 said that the Spirit of the Lord came on David from that day forward.

For whatever reason, when David stood there and listened to Goliath's taunts, he was not afraid. In fact, a righteous indignation rose up within him. Not so with the other Israelites. They were dreadfully afraid, terrified, panic-stricken. They scattered, running for their lives in all directions.

David didn't just listen and think about what he had heard. He used his mouth too—we call it attitude today.

Yes, David had an attitude! In fact, along with his righteous indignation, he had a "violent spirit." He lifted up his voice and asked the Israelites who were still standing around him:

> What's in it for the man who kills that Philistine and gets rid of this ugly blot on Israel's honor? Who does he think he is, anyway, this uncircumcised Philistine, taunting the armies of God-Alive?
>
> —1 SAMUEL 17:26, THE MESSAGE

Were David's words the epitome of presumption? He was an unlikely hero. At least that's what his brothers thought. Who was this teenaged pip-squeak, mouthing off? His oldest brother decided to strip their sibling down to size with his words. (Is there not usually someone standing by who attempts to reduce you to size when you become confident?)

> Eliab, his older brother, heard David fraternizing with the men and lost his temper: "What are you doing here! Why aren't you minding your own business, tending that scrawny flock of sheep? I know what you're up to. You've come down here to see the sights, hoping for a ringside seat at a bloody battle!"
>
> —1 Samuel 17:28, The Message

David shot back, "What is it with you?...All I did was ask a question" (v. 29). But Saul got wind of what David was saying and called for him.

There are times when someone is going to hear what you are saying even though everyone around you thinks you are crazy for saying it. God will cause that person to hear the right words, at the right time, and they will call for you. Only God can set these situations up.

King Saul took David up on his boast. He put him out there to face off with Goliath.

Remember, it wasn't just because David was boastful. Realistically, he had qualified to face off with Goliath because he had proven his mettle. He had demonstrated that he had guts. He was prepared. One of the things he explained to Saul was that he had already defeated a lion and a bear. To David, Goliath was just another challenge in a continuing string of challenges.

Why had he taken on the lion and the bear? They were trying to take the lambs. You and I must first learn to care deeply about the seemingly insignificant matters and about people, about a little lamb, a new Christian struggling in the spiritual life. David had a heart not just for the big things but also for the ordinary, small things that mattered.

King Saul was impressed. He gave David his backing, and he tried to give him his own armor and a sword; however, David preferred his own clothes.

David gathered up five smooth stones from the bed of the brook and put them in his shepherd's pack. With his sling in one hand and his shepherd's staff in the other, he approached Goliath, who was waiting for him in the hot sun. David, the warrior-shepherd went into the battle with righteous indignation (a slingshot) and a shepherd's heart for God's people (his shepherd's staff).

> As the Philistine paced back and forth, his shield bearer in front of him, he noticed David. He took one look down on him and sneered—a mere youngster, apple-cheeked and peach-fuzzed. The Philistine ridiculed David. "Am I a dog that you come after me with a stick?" And he cursed him by his gods. "Come on," said the Philistine. "I'll make roadkill of you for the buzzards. I'll turn you into a tasty morsel for the field mice."
>
> —1 Samuel 17:41–44, The Message

"Inciteful" Words

David's words are critically important here. I once heard a well-known speaker say, "If you don't feel it, fake it! It's your words that are so critical." Whether David was faking it or not, he spoke out confidently:

> You come at me with sword and spear and battle-ax. I come at you in the name of God-of-the-Angel-Armies, the God of Israel's troops, whom you curse and mock. This very day God is handing you over to me. I'm about to kill you, cut off your head, and serve up your body and the bodies of your Philistine buddies to the crows and coyotes. The whole earth will know

that there's an extraordinary God in Israel. And everyone gathered here will learn that God doesn't save by means of sword or spear. The battle belongs to God—he's handing you to us on a platter!

—1 SAMUEL 17:45–47, THE MESSAGE

Those words did it. They incited Goliath to fight. He shifted his weight and moved threateningly toward David.

Did that make David take a step backward? I don't think so!

In fact, David ran toward him! He took the offensive, not the defensive.

And you know, as the giant came toward him head-on, it was good thing that David was not encumbered by Saul's heavy armor. He was wearing his normal, light shepherd's clothing. In other words, he went to battle in his own identity. David's clothing was so light, and because he was young, he was nimble-footed. It didn't matter what Goliath did. David could dance around Goliath's moves.

For each of us there will be times when we need to run toward our enemy, knowing that the battle belongs to the Lord. We have to come out of our prayer closets and out of our strategizing, talking, conceptualizing, formulating, and procrastinating. We need to *engage*. We need to face off with the enemy weapon to weapon, word to word.

ONE SMALL STONE—A KINGDOM-KILLER

David reached into his shepherd's pack, pulled out one of the smooth stones, and placed it into his slingshot. He began to swing the sling: *Whoosh! Whoosh! Whoosh!*

Meanwhile, Goliath gloated. He thought this was ridiculous, an insult even. Little did Goliath know that *Whoosh! Whoosh! Whoosh!* was the sound of his defeat. It was the sound of victory for David.

There is a sound of war, of engagement in battle, that will defeat the enemy. It can come through worship, through our own voice, through a CD, through a child. Listen for that sound and move forward; take the next step when the sound ignites your spirit with faith.

Suddenly David released the stone. It hit its mark—right in the middle of Goliath's forehead—and the Philistine crashed facedown in the dirt. The Philistines were in an uproar. When they saw that their hero was dead, they ran for their lives.

David wasn't carrying a sword himself, you will remember, but he ran up to the fallen giant and took the giant's own sword right out of its sheath, lopping Goliath's head off to bring to Jerusalem as a trophy (1 Sam. 17:50–51). In one stroke, he removed the headship, ruling power, and authority of all that Goliath stood for. That day not only did David defeat Goliath, who represented the demonic stronghold that held the Israelites captive, but he also defeated a kingdom.

It's the same for us. When we defeat Goliaths, entire kingdoms are defeated and the spoils are delivered into our hands. The enemy flees, and the kingdom of God moves in.

ONE SMALL STONE—A MIGHTY KINGDOM

David began to rule as a warrior from that day forward. He was known nationwide as a warrior well before he ascended the throne to rule as king over the people of Israel. On that single day when he defeated Goliath, he began to rule—over the enemy.

So it is today, when God is raising up and revealing Davids who can deliver kingdoms into the hands of the church of Jesus Christ. We are living in a day when God is thrusting His Davids into public arenas to deal with the Goliaths of our nation as well as the nations of the earth.

Kings rule kingdoms, but a process is required for a king to arise. That process begins with the role of the warrior. Spiritual warriors learn to take territories, nations, and kingdoms. They learn to possess what belongs to God. They understand what a kingdom is, they see how they are unseated and established, and they know which part of the kingdom they are assigned to. They know their sphere of authority.

Kingdoms are arenas that are governed by a leader. David had been handed authority when Samuel anointed him as king. His authority began to be demonstrated with Goliath.

Over time, he had to grow into the full use of his authority when the people recognized him as king and called for him to be enthroned. Eventually David overcame every last enemy of Israel.

With the taking of the city of Jerusalem, David overcame the Jebusites who were the last enemy, the holdouts. At that point the people gathered to David and completed his ascension to the throne. They made him king not only over Israel but also over Judah. He attained total rulership.

A KINGDOM THAT OVERCOMES EVERY OTHER KINGDOM

So David started as a warrior and continued steadfastly until he became the recognized king over a united kingdom. God spoke of the significance of his throne, declaring that his kingdom would be established forever. (See 2 Samuel 7:13, 16.) That small stone David used to kill Goliath went on to overcome every other kingdom. It was representative of both a people and a kingdom that was to come.

In Daniel 2, we read of another stone that became a kingdom. This is Daniel's interpretation of one of Nebuchadnezzar's dreams:

> And in the days of these [final ten] kings shall the God of heaven set up a kingdom which shall never be destroyed, nor shall its sovereignty be left to another people; but it shall break and crush and consume all these kingdoms and it shall stand forever. Just as you saw that the Stone was cut out of the mountain without hands and that it broke in pieces the iron, the bronze, the clay, the silver, and the gold, the great God has made known to the king what shall come to pass hereafter. The dream is certain and the interpretation of it is sure.
>
> —DANIEL 2:44–45, AMP

In both cases, David's small stone and the stone cut out of the mountain, a small, seemingly insignificant stone, went on to become a kingdom that would overcome every other kingdom.

In Scripture, "kingdoms" are often identified as mountains. This picture of a stone cut from a mountain declares prophetically that God's kingdom will increase progressively in size, stature, authority, and power, eventually shattering every other kingdom. David's kingdom is to continue forever through Jesus Christ, the Son of God.

> For unto us a Child is born, unto us a Son is given; and the government will be upon His shoulder. And His name will be called Wonderful, Counselor, Mighty God, Everlasting Father, Prince of Peace. Of the increase of His government and peace there will be no end, upon the throne of David and over His kingdom, to order it and establish it with judgment and justice

from that time forward, even forever. The zeal of the Lord of hosts will perform this.

—ISAIAH 9:6–7

Jesus came to create the way through which this could be fulfilled. Through His life, death, and resurrection, He became the King of kings, the Lord of lords. He came to sit on the throne of David, to establish it with judgment and justice, to rule forever. That mountain, that kingdom, is to overcome every other kingdom.

But Jesus was not only a king; He remained a warrior:

Now I saw heaven opened, and behold, a white horse. And He who sat on him was called Faithful and True, and in righteousness He judges and makes war. His eyes were like a flame of fire, and on His head were many crowns. He had a name written that no one knew except Himself. He was clothed with a robe dipped in blood, and His name is called The Word of God. And the armies in heaven, clothed in fine linen, white and clean, followed Him on white horses. Now out of His mouth goes a sharp sword, that with it He should strike the nations. And He Himself will rule them with a rod of iron. He Himself treads the winepress of the fierceness and wrath of Almighty God. And He has on His robe and on His thigh a name written: KING OF KINGS AND LORD OF LORDS.

—REVELATION 19:11–16

This is Jesus, our warrior King.

In his letter to the Ephesians, the apostle Paul talks about how Jesus became both the King of kings and Lord of lords and the warrior King. He expounds magnificently on the work of God through Jesus Christ, who overcame every power, and all authority and rule, and then went on to assume the headship of the church. Furthermore, Paul tells us how Jesus made the church (that's you and me) into His delegated body to enforce His rule on the earth, releasing and advancing His kingdom.

You and I are to become like Jesus, warriors and types of kings who rule and reign in the arena God has delivered into our hands. As Paul asked:

> I pray that the eyes of your heart may be enlightened, so that you will know what is the hope of His calling, what are the riches of the glory of His inheritance in the saints, and what is the surpassing greatness of His power toward us who believe. These are in accordance with the working of the strength of His might which He brought about in Christ, when He raised Him from the dead and seated Him at His right hand in the heavenly places, far above all rule and authority and power and dominion, and every name that is named, not only in this age but also in the one to come. And He put all things in subjection under His feet, and gave Him as head over all things to the church, which is His body, the fullness of Him who fills all in all.
>
> —EPHESIANS 1:18–23, NAS

ONE SMALL STONE

This gets even better! Hold on to your chair. In his first letter, the apostle Peter quotes Isaiah 28:16 and Psalm 118:22. He writes of Jesus:

> Behold, I lay in Zion a chief cornerstone, elect, precious, and he who believes on Him will by no means be put to shame.... The

stone which the builders rejected has become the chief cornerstone.

—1 PETER 2:6–7

Just before this verse, the apostle Peter wrote about you and me. He called us "living stones." In the mind of God, you and I are stones:

Coming to Him as to a living stone, rejected indeed by men, but chosen by God and precious, you also, as living stones, are being built up a spiritual house, a holy priesthood, to offer up spiritual sacrifices acceptable to God through Jesus Christ.

—1 PETER 2:4–5

In other words, Jesus is the chief cornerstone—the "stone cut out of the mountain"—and you and I are separate small stones, chosen by God, precious and alive. Together we form a house, a kingdom, a spiritual force on the earth.

Could it be that now, through us, God is continuing what David began by hurling one small stone against Goliath? Could it be that you and I individually are stones that are being hurled at each of our Goliaths?

God is continuing to war against the powers of darkness and to establish His kingdom in the earth. He is doing it through individuals. We are warriors, meant to be hurled both individually and corporately at the giants who rule kingdoms of darkness today.

We have been released as giant-killing stones. We have been released as God's spiritual forces. You and I and every other believer, each of us, are destined to become giant-killers like David.

6

The Violent Spirit

THIS SCRIPTURE LEAPS OFF THE PAGE AND STRIKES me on my head like an ill-placed baseball bat swing. These words sound scary!

And from the days of John the Baptist until now the kingdom of heaven suffers violence, and the violent take it by force.

—MATTHEW 11:12

I know we live in an age of violent radicalization of religious forces. Islam has terrorism as its modus operandi, seeking world domination through fear, trying to force nations to bow to Islamic rule. We also have militia groups in the United States, homebred and homegrown, who advocate the taking up of arms and violence to bring about change. Some of them claim they are Christians, and yet their focus is the promotion of the supposedly superior white people above any other ethnic group or race, which makes them no different from Hitler or other supremacists throughout history.

Does Christianity promote that kind of violence to protect the kingdom of heaven and to enforce its "superiority"? Is that what Matthew 11:12 means?

No! The use of the words *violence* and *violent* should not be interpreted that way. This passage is about an entirely different issue.

I like the way the New International Version translates the same verse: "From the days of John the Baptist until now, the kingdom of heaven has been forcefully advancing, and forceful men lay hold of it." Instead of "violence," the NIV uses the phrase "forcefully advancing." Forceful advancing implies a forward-moving, territory-taking struggle over who is in control, an effort to change the command structure.

Repent, for the Kingdom
of Heaven Is at Hand

Consider the prevailing mission of John the Baptist. He called men to repent because the kingdom of heaven was at hand. In other words, if people wanted to become part of the kingdom that was coming into the world through Jesus—which was the kingdom of heaven—the first thing they had to do was to change their minds about who was in control.

Repentance is not complicated. It is not even particularly emotional, although most people interpret it emotionally, assuming it means to cry uncontrollably because of having committed some sin. Even when people respond emotionally, repentance is not an emotional issue; it is a spiritual one. To repent simply means to change one's mind, to make an about-face or to turn and go in a different direction.

The rich young ruler provides a negative example of repentance. We can read his story in Luke 18:18–27. His problem was not immorality, murder, stealing, dishonoring his parents, or maligning people's reputations. His quandary was that he loved money more than he loved God. Nonetheless, he wanted to inherit eternal life. To do so, Jesus told the rich ruler that he must give his money to the poor.

The young man couldn't do it. He could not repent or change his mind. He preferred to maintain the dominance of his wealth.

As a result, Jesus responded that it is very difficult for people with riches to enter the kingdom of God. They live in the kingdom of their own wealth. They maintain their own sense of control through wealth. They are self-dependent.

The disciples asked Jesus, "Who then can be saved?" (v. 26). I imagine that they identified with the rich young ruler, don't you? Jesus responded that with man this is impossible, out of the question, like threading a camel through the eye of a needle. But He said that with God, all things are possible. God can enable us to repent.

Paul said that it is the goodness of God that leads us to repentance (Rom. 2:4). The word *goodness* in the Greek has a root word that means "to furnish what is needed," or to "light upon." God, through His Holy Spirit, furnishes you and me with what is needed, the necessary conviction to break through to repentance. He also lights upon us, falls upon us, overcomes us, so that we can repent. It all goes back to God.

Why did John tell the people to repent to prepare the way of the Lord? Because they could not have it both ways—their way and God's way. They had to surrender to God. They had to give up their own way.

Repentance is a control or a "throne" issue. When I repent, I give up the right of rulership to my life. Who will rule my life? By default, sin will. Sin in any form is simply the failure to follow God and His Word, to submit to His kingship, and thereby to become part of His kingdom.

Repentance is the entry point, the ticket, to the kingdom of God. But once we are residents in God's kingdom, the issue changes to an ownership one. For whom and what will we fight now? We used to fight for our own rights. Now we must be willing to fight for God's kingdom.

WHAT IS A KINGDOM?

A kingdom is a realm of rule. It is a physical or defined territory with boundaries over which a ruler has been placed. A nation is a type of kingdom. A corporation is a type of kingdom. A family is a mini-kingdom.

Kingdoms are politically organized communities or major territorial units that have a monarchical form of government headed by a king (or queen). A kingdom is a realm, region, area, or sphere in which someone or something is preeminent or dominant. In old England, the king or the queen was dominant. In the animal kingdom, animals are dominant. In the kingdom of God, God is dominant.

The passage in Matthew concerns the kingdom of *God*. In this kingdom, God asserts His control through His "armed forces," if you will. Just as nations, which are kingdoms, are willing to go to war for the purpose of protecting their national interests, and they have armies employed for this very purpose, so does God. He has His angels, and He has His church. And that's where we come in.

In other words, not only are we citizens, but we are also the *armed forces* of the kingdom of God. We must be willing to take whatever action is needed to enforce, to defend, and to advance the kingdom of God.

JOHN THE BAPTIST, KINGDOM-ADVANCER

Go back to John the Baptist, who was unrelenting in preaching his message of, "Repent, for the kingdom of heaven is at hand!" (Matt. 3:2). He harped on this message. When people did repent, he then baptized them. Somehow that baptism washed away a film from their spiritual eyes. The Bible indicates that John's baptism was so powerful in its spiritual dynamic that people who had been baptized by John were able to perceive Jesus's significance when He came. (See Luke 7:29–30.)

I assume that John the Baptist only took time away from "crying out" while he was baptizing the people who had received his message. The rest of the time he kept crying out, heralding a message to repent.

This was extreme! It was what today most people would call fanatical. This man was glued to his message like a fly to flypaper. Why? Because he had seen something; he had heard something that had become a part of him. He had a mission, a purpose, something to accomplish. He did not get off task. He was unrelenting in his pursuit of the goal that was set before him. He kept pressing the issue.

John was a voice. He cried out in the middle of the wilderness, the place between the exit and the entrance, which is the place of transition, and he said, "Prepare the way of the Lord; make His paths straight" (Matt. 3:3). His voice, crying out in the transitional place, aligned people with what was about to come, which was new.

He prepared the way for God to come in an all-new way. He risked everything and gave up life as he had known it to become a wandering voice that called people into a new place. "Repent, for the kingdom of heaven is at hand. Make way for the King!"

FORTY YEARS

Remember the Israelites. They were delivered out of Egypt so that they could go to Canaan. But they ended up staying in the wilderness for a long and difficult forty years rather than a mere eleven days, all because of their disobedience.

They were afraid to take a risk. The cost and the consequences seemed too extreme. So they resisted moving from the wilderness to

Canaan, which God had promised them, remaining in the transitional, wilderness place for forty years—until the whole generation died off.

They did not enter Canaan because they were afraid. Crossing the threshold into Canaan would have required them to "forcefully advance." They chose to stay where they were. That whole generation was not "violent" enough.

PRESSING THROUGH

The apostle Paul didn't hesitate like that. He kept pressing on to lay hold of that for which God had laid hold of him:

> I press on to take hold of that for which Christ Jesus took hold of me. Brothers, I do not consider myself yet to have taken hold of it. But one thing I do: Forgetting what is behind and straining toward what is ahead, I press on toward the goal to win the prize for which God has called me heavenward in Christ Jesus.
> —PHILIPPIANS 3:12–14, NIV

Paul did not deviate, take detours, or hem and haw. He stayed on task, pursuing the goal unrelentingly. I believe he was doing what Matthew 11:12 describes: pressing into, forcefully advancing.

VIOLENCE, VIOLENT, FORCE

What do the words *violence, violent,* and *force* mean? As I have outlined, most versions of Matthew 11:12 use "violence," "the violent," "forcefully advancing," and "forceful men." The Living Bible, however, interprets the wording like this: "And from the time John the Baptist began preaching and baptizing until now, ardent multitudes have been crowding toward the Kingdom of Heaven."

This version provides another image of a forceful and even violent advance. Here we see that the people are *crowding* toward their goal of the kingdom of heaven. Other words that have been used to interpret the Greek terminology include "pressing toward" and "seizing something." This pressing, seizing, and crowding forward is very energetic. People need to exert some effort in their approach toward the kingdom.

Webster's New World Dictionary defines *violence* as:

1. Exerting any force so as to enter something that is closed off. It can be abusive, injurious, warfare, or something that affects the entry into something.

2. Intense, turbulent, or furious action, force, or feeling

3. Vehement feeling or expression—fervor, passion, fury

4. A clashing, jarring, discordant, or abrupt quality

5. The intense show of action or feeling

According to Webster's, *violent* also means extremely or intensely vivid or loud. It means to be vehement to the point of being improper, to be unusually intense or passionate.

All of these definitions can apply to John the Baptist. He was pressing into something, forcing his way through obstacles so as to release his message to the largest number of individuals possible. He wanted to make sure that everyone heard the message that Jesus was coming. He was compelled to prepare the way for Him by compelling people to seize a truth. He pressed his message home, and he exerted great energy or effort in order to accomplish that.

COMPELLED, COMPELLING

Paul told the Corinthians that "the love of Christ *compels* us" (2 Cor. 5:14). The Amplified Bible states it this way: "For the love of Christ controls and urges and impels us, because we are of the opinion and conviction that [if] One died for all, then all died."

Can you sense the energy, the drive, the force, the pressing toward something? Paul was "violent" in his love toward the Corinthians.

In the same way, John the Baptist was compelling and passionate about his message. He was passionate even to the point of seeming improper. He was vehement. Consider this outburst:

> Brood of vipers! Who warned you to flee from the wrath to come? Therefore bear fruits worthy of repentance, and do not think to say to yourselves, "We have Abraham as our father." For I say to you that God is able to raise up children to Abraham from these stones. And even now the ax is laid to the root of the trees. Therefore every tree which does not bear good fruit is cut down and thrown into the fire. I indeed baptize you with water unto repentance, but He who is coming after me is mightier than I, whose sandals I am not worthy to carry. He will baptize you with the Holy Spirit and fire. His winnowing fan is in His hand, and He will thoroughly clean out His threshing floor, and gather His wheat into the barn; but He will burn up the chaff with unquenchable fire.
>
> —Matthew 3:7–12

He was intense, passionate, energetic, forceful, compelling, and discomforting. A passion rose from the depths of his spirit, and he was driven by it. He *had* to make something happen.

Defending Territory

It's not hard for me to understand these concepts when I think about my little eleven-pound dog. Her name is Missy. However small and prissy she appears to be is irrelevant, for inside her head she is the queen, the ruling monarch of my property. It does not make a bit of difference how big the dog might be who passes through my yard. That dog automatically becomes a trespasser of Missy's kingdom, her territory, her physical sphere of rule.

One day this huge dog walked across the sidewalk in front of the house. Missy happened to be unleashed. She took off like a rocket toward that animal that was at least the size of a Saint Bernard. She yipped furiously and attacked him so fiercely that he never had time to remember that he was many times bigger than she was. He ran off down the street faster than I thought any big dog's legs could take him.

You see, Missy has a complete understanding of who she is and what her mission in life is. It compels her to action no matter how big the task or how daunting the foe. She is not intimidated in the least. In this one regard, she has a totally violent spirit, and she presses every trespasser into submission.

Violence has to be characterized by extreme force. Think of a violent storm, which can arise with abnormal suddenness and unusual intensity—vivid lightning, clashing thunder, beating rain. Sometimes, like a violent storm, something just rises up inside us. Like Missy, we fly into action without thinking. We exercise our godly authority and stomp on the head of the enemy, regardless of how strong he appears to be.

Last summer it happened, once again, to me. I got a phone call from a person who had been very sick for a long time. I had known about it, I prayed about it, but nothing changed. Suddenly, I had had enough of this sickness. Something rose up in me, and I said, "In the authority of Jesus's name, you disease that is trying to steal Jessie's* health and liberty, I command you to loose her and let her go."

And it happened! Just as suddenly as I commanded it to leave, her sickness left. I didn't even think about it. I didn't worry about coaching her ahead of time—"Well, you know, I'm thinking of doing something that might just be a little expressive or intense." No, I just exploded with violence on her behalf. It was instant warfare, and it broke through the sickness barrier.

It was time for a breakthrough. Something got into my backbone. I couldn't tolerate the situation for one more moment. Something inside me burst out, "Enough is enough!"

Do you know what I'm talking about? Has it happened to you?

When it happens, you don't harm the other person. But in that moment, you are far from being a "nice," passionless Christian. You aren't responding like an abuser, with anger toward the person. You are responding like a warrior, in defense of the person. Something or someone has been violated, and you won't stand by and watch it happen anymore.

If someone came in and tried to kidnap your child, would you say, "Oh, I'm a Christian, so I cannot hurt you, but will you please give me back my child?" No, you would react so fast the kidnapper wouldn't know what had happened.

One time when I was speaking at a conference, I was informed that a friend's child had disappeared. All of a sudden, while preaching, I spoke out authoritatively, saying, "I command you to let Janna* go. Angels, go

---

* Not her real name

and bring Janna home." That was a type of violence. My friend's child returned home within a couple of days.

God's Warriors Have a Violent Spirit

Can you imagine how it would be if the church were to arise and become "violent"? You and I are the church. We are the ones whom God is challenging to arise, to see, to stand, to advance, to push through whatever is holding back the fullness of the expression of Christ in a given arena.

True warriors have a violent spirit, as I already defined. You and I are called to be warriors. We are to fight for something God has put into our hearts. We are part of the generation that is supposed to work and fight to see change.

Each of us has assignments. We are called to work together in our assigned arenas; for you it may be one thing, for me another. I have a friend who contends for families, another for the unborn. Some are in government; others are in the schools and in corporations. One friend contends for young people who have been waylaid by drugs, alcohol, fatherlessness, sex, and civil infractions. Each of these friends is a warrior, and each of them has a warring spirit.

True warriors who possess a violent spirit are those who exert a force to try to enter into something that is closed off. They have a breaker anointing to break through every obstacle and gate and hindrance to the kingdom of God. When violence in warfare comes upon them, they are intense, even turbulent and furious. They are passionate for the kingdom of God.

A PASSIONLESS PEOPLE?

Some have observed that America as a whole has become passionless. They predict that this nation will no longer be willing to go to war because we have been spoiled by abundance and have been seduced to sleep by comfort.

A year or so ago I attended a private lecture presented by an Arab gentleman who happened to be Islamic. I am not free to give his name, but, in his lecture, he stated that America as a nation does not want to pay the price of war to retain its freedom. He further said that American citizens have lost the passion they once had, and, therefore, they could now be conquered. He felt that the whole country had lost its passion to fight for what is right.

In an article posted on the Web, author Karlyn Bowman quoted David Gergen in calling Americans "the passionless public." Here is part of what she wrote:

> In a panel discussion at the American Enterprise Institute on the first 100 days of the Bush presidency, David Gergen suggested that what we might have today is a "passionless public." "The public," he said, "has been extraordinarily disengaged from many of the conversations that have been taking place in Washington, and that follows a pattern we saw in foreign policy when [Bill] Clinton was president." In coining the term, Gergen recalled James Fallows's 1979 articles on Jimmy Carter as the passionless president. Gergen went on to say that the public seems to be saying, "...don't bother me in my life." There's a lot of poll evidence to support his assessment.[1]

I've thought a lot about that—the absence of passion. I don't want to be lulled to sleep by the culture around me, but has it happened? Have you been influenced by the culture? Can you measure your own passion?

WEAPONS OF INDIGNATION

More than a year ago, Pastor Ken Malone, the Global Apostolic Prayer Network leader for the state of Florida, invited me to present a vision for prayer on a national teleconference call that he would moderate. I was to speak for about fifteen to twenty minutes, and then the intercessory panel from across the nation would pray along the lines of my presentation.

As I was preparing for the teleconference earlier that day, I prayed, and the Lord spoke a word to my heart. He told me I should "stir up the weapons of indignation." That made me ask the question: "What *are* the weapons of indignation? Are they actual weapons or something else?"

I found part of my answer in two different Scripture passages, both of which mention weapons of indignation. One is from the Book of Isaiah:

> The burden against Babylon which Isaiah the son of Amoz saw. "Lift up a banner on the high mountain, raise your voice to them; wave your hand, that they may enter the gates of the nobles. I have commanded My sanctified ones; I have also called My mighty ones for My anger—those who rejoice in My exaltation." The noise of a multitude in the mountains, like that of many people! A tumultuous noise of the kingdoms of nations gathered together! The Lord of hosts musters the army for battle. They come from a far country, from the end of

heaven—the Lord and His *weapons of indignation*, to destroy
the whole land.

—ISAIAH 13:1–5, EMPHASIS ADDED

This passage shows that both the Lord and His people, His army,
have been taken over by a violent spirit. Something has so incensed
God, and also those who have His heart, that they are arising as an
army to deal with something that is wrong, evil, and sinful.

In other words, the Lord's weapons of indignation are *people*. People
have become the weapons in His hand. They are being used to open up
something that is closed off. They are being used to cut off something
that has risen up to destroy the nation. Theirs is an indignant spirit,
a violent spirit. It rages at something that is totally wrong, something
that destroys people's well-being, something that does damage to their
ability to thrive spiritually.

Then I looked at Jeremiah 50:25:

> The LORD has opened His armory, and has brought out the
> *weapons of His indignation*; for this is the work of the Lord
> God of hosts.

—EMPHASIS ADDED

Here again, you see that the weapons of indignation don't come from
a military arsenal. God's weapons of indignation are individual people
who have become angry about an injustice. Together, they form *armies*
of indignation. They channel their passion toward a goal. They defend
righteousness. They get mad at the things they should get mad at. They
present a united front of holy, righteous indignation in action.

People who are indignant are angry. This isn't a bad thing. Psychia-
trists will tell you that they would rather have somebody who is angry

come into their office than somebody who is passive. When they come in angry, it shows that they still have feelings. But if they come in passive, it means they have shut down and are going to need someone's help to find their passion before they can be motivated to make changes.

Oftentimes, in the case of warfare, you have to get mad enough about a situation to get out there to change it. You have to get mad enough at being poor, mad enough at being abused, mad enough about someone transgressing boundaries, mad enough to take up a righteous cause and see it through to victory. You rise up in a spirit of holy contentiousness and you *contend*—as I have already mentioned—as long as it takes to achieve complete success.

Are you one of God's weapons of indignation? If not, you can be.

WHAT IS "FORCE"?

Remember, the New King James Version of Matthew 11:12 states, "...the kingdom of heaven suffers violence, and the violent take it *by force*" (emphasis added). What does by "force" mean?

Force is active power, vigor, strength. To take something by force is to take it by exerting strength or energy of an exceptional degree. It means to overcome resistance by using strength or power, often combined with the strength of other people. Force includes moral or mental strength, which enables a person to overcome the power of their opposition.

Not to be confused with the negative kind of violence that is involved in physical assault, it is also the power or capacity to sway, to convince. This kind of force releases spiritual change in a family, neighborhood, church, business, school, government, or even a nation.

People who exercise this force have real authority from heaven, not merely a title or position. If they are leaders, they need to possess an unusual degree of moral and mental strength.

We all know that just because a person is a leader does not guarantee that he or she is "great." Leaders can have strength of character and godliness—or they can be wimpy. The ones who are able to compel positive change have not only the authority that comes with their title but also a strength of character that is imparted by God.

A force is also a large quantity or number of something. What do we call the combined branches of the United States defense services? We call them our "armed forces." The armed forces are people who form the main defense, the strength, of a nation.

Could it be that we, you and I, are to be the armed forces of God? We don't have to do it in our own human strength; God will endow us with supernatural wisdom, strategies, and perseverance. His militant angels will rise up in response to our holy indignation.

UNSTOPPABLE

In the foreword of the book *An Unstoppable Force: Daring to Become the Church God Had in Mind,* Brad Smith wrote that the book would create an abrupt opening of the window shade, revealing that we all had been hitting the snooze button for decades.[2] In other words, he is saying that we have been choosing comfort rather than making the hard decisions—such as becoming a member of "the force"—kingdom enforcers and kingdom advancers. Some of the greatest kingdom advancers contend with evil powers for a long time before they win, but their perseverance makes them unstoppable.

A good example of that kind of untiring force was a young Lutheran pastor named Johann Christoph Blumhardt, who lived in Mottlingen, Germany, in the nineteenth century. Educated but inexperienced, he encountered two young women who were sisters—and they were demonized.

They acted normal and nice part of the time, but then they would sort of space out and contort and have other demonic manifestations. Blumhardt had no training in deliverance. Nevertheless he began to contend with the unseen powers that controlled not only the two women but also, it seemed, the whole town as well.

For two years, he contended with the demonic powers. He didn't stop. He didn't consider it an experiment. He just kept contending until he broke through. Altogether he cast out more than a thousand demons from the women. And at the end of the two years, a decisive confrontation occurred. When the very last demon was cast out of the two sisters, it left with a loud cry, "Jesus is victor!"

At that moment, not only were the women transformed and set free, but also the powers that had held the town in bondage were finally broken. The people began to shout the same words: "Jesus is victor!"

That was the beginning of an awakening in that town that lasted for years. It happened all because of a man who kept forcefully advancing. He was unstoppable. He refused to stop until he saw complete victory.[3]

Johann Christoph Blumhardt had a violent spirit that would not let go or give up, no matter how long and contentious the struggle. His determination advanced the kingdom of God and changed the spiritual climate in his sphere of authority. He exemplifies a kind of contending that is like travail. The breakthrough may not get completed in a day or two, or even in a month or two, but it keeps on happening until the "baby" is born.

WHAT IS GOD DOING NOW?

Why am I telling you all this? Could it be that God is about to open His armory to loose the weapons of His indignation with greater intensity and frequency? Can it be that He is going to awaken more people to the need? Does that include you?

Has He already opened up His armory and brought out some of His weapons of indignation? I believe that Martin Luther King Jr. and those who marched with him were weapons of indignation. These men and women arose as a mighty army to turn the laws of the land, defeating segregation. They arose as an army, not with guns, grenades, or mortar shells, but with a passion that made them unstoppable.

In their kind of "violence," they arose and marched peacefully. They were compelled to march, no matter what the white men—or any race—might say, until their people were freed from segregation.

In the same battle, Rosa Parks was another weapon of indignation. Something got into her that made this African American woman refuse to move to the back of the bus that day in Montgomery, Alabama. Her action touched off a revolution.

In the present day, could it be that part of God's army can be seen on the evening news? Do you remember when Lou Engle and his gathering of young people took their stand near the steps to the U.S. Supreme Court building in Washington DC during the partial-birth abortion hearings? The youth covered their mouths with red tape and printed the word *LIFE* on that tape. The tape represented the silent cries of the unborn babies who have been aborted, whose voices have been shut up, shut off, and done away with forever in this life.

Those young people were standing before the Supreme Court of the United States of America to make a statement and take a stand. By their actions, they were saying, "Overturn the abortion decisions in America. Change the laws of this land. We will stand here, and we will not be moved. We have become weapons of indignation, and now we have become a force before the Supreme Court."

These young people were determined and defiant but also courageous and peaceful. They didn't care if they got arrested or hurt. Incorporated into their forceful, persistent indignation was a willingness to die for their own agenda, comfort, and preferences, perhaps even to die physically as a martyr.

I asked my granddaughter Tarrah to say something about this. She is an administrative assistant to the Israel Department at Eagles' Wings Ministries, in Clarence, New York, serving under the director Robert Stearns. She wrote:

What many people are rarely told but soon find out is that in the fine print the "chosen generation" has a great price to pay. So few are willing to pay it.

I was always told that I had a great calling on my life, that I would change the world. It sounded wonderful and fulfilling. But what people failed to tell me was that I would have to die. I would have to die to myself in order to fulfill a call that was greater than myself. In fact, I could not respond to the call to be a warrior if I was not willing to die. "Precious in the sight of the Lord is the death of His saints" (Ps. 116:15).

The world tells us to desire popularity, fame, fortune. But the Bible tells us we must die so that we can live. I find Jesus's words show the first step in a warrior's journey: "And he who does not take his cross and follow after Me is not worthy of Me. He who finds his life will lose it, and he who loses his life for My sake will find it" (Matt. 10:38–39).

SONS OF ISSACHAR

In order to follow God into battle formation, we need to be as discerning as the sons of Issachar, who served to help make David the king of Israel.

> Now these were the numbers of the divisions that were equipped for war, and came to David at Hebron to turn over the kingdom of Saul to him, according to the word of the LORD ... of the children of Issachar who had understanding of the times, to know what Israel ought to do, their chiefs were two hundred; and all their brethren were at their command. ... All these men of war, who could keep ranks, came to Hebron with a loyal heart, to make David king over all Israel; and all the rest of Israel were of one mind to make David king.
>
> —1 CHRONICLES 12:23, 32, 38

We see that they were armed for war, and they were trained and prepared, "stouthearted men who could keep ranks" (v. 33), men who knew how to use "every kind of weapon of war" (v. 37). They were "mighty men of valor, famous men throughout their father's house" (v. 30).

They knew what to do, and they weren't afraid to do it. They were fully united with others who were like-minded, who were passionate for their cause and courageous in the face of opposition.

What is your cause? Do you know yet? Do you possess a warrior's violent, forceful spirit? Are you undergoing training and preparation, or are you already on the battlefield? You too can be an unstoppable force in the hand of the living God. You are getting your induction papers. Will you accept the charge?

7

Faith That Speaks, Creates

MY AUNT WAS DYING. I WAS A YOUNG Christian, growing in my walk with God, recently baptized in the Holy Spirit. A whole new world had opened up to me, one in which miracles happened.

I loved my aunt, who was only in her early fifties, and I could not believe that she would die so young. She had smoked most of her adult life, and cigarettes had taken their toll on her lungs. Yet was not God the God of the impossible?

I was sure God did not want her to die. I was convinced that He would heal her. So I began to pray for her.

One day, I felt I had broken through to the heart of God for my aunt. I felt sure that if I laid my hands on her in prayer, she would be healed. Didn't the Word say that we should lay hands on the sick and they would recover? So I bought a plane ticket to Madison, Wisconsin, in order to pray for her in person.

My father met me at the airport with tears in his eyes. He was so glad that I had come and that I believed God was going to heal his sister. Together we rejoiced, expecting God to work a miracle. Carrying my bag, he walked me to his car. He and my stepmother had driven up from Indianapolis to be with his sister, as they had been doing every other weekend.

I wanted my aunt to be healed as much for my father's sake as for my aunt's sake. I didn't want him to be hurt anymore. He had already lost both his wife (my mother) and his parents to death, all within the same month. Surely God would not also take away his beloved sister.

PAST VICTORIES

We arrived at the hospital. There was my aunt in the bed, frail and clearly in the last days of her bout with cancer. It mattered not, because I had *faith*. A few family members, including her son, were with her, and we gathered around her bed.

While waiting together, I brought to mind some of my past experiences with God's healing. There was the time I had laid hands on my stepmother and she had been healed of a serious kidney infection. That was the first time I prayed for a family member, and I had been anxious about it. We didn't *do* that in our family, and I wasn't used to praying for the sick. But I felt God had said, "Lay hands on her and pray for her." So in blind obedience, I did so.

After praying, I left to see a friend. I wasn't very sure that God was going to heal my stepmother, and I didn't want to be there if she wasn't healed. In spite of my low faith level, however, God did heal her. I'm not sure *my* faith was involved at all, but I do know obedience was. From that, I realized an important principle: God is true to His Word, not mine. He had simply honored His own Word when I followed it.

Then there was the time God had healed me of bronchitis. For years, I had bouts of it at least two, sometimes three times a year. One night I could feel it coming on. I happened to be in a car with a group of nuns. I told them about it, and we began to sing and praise the Lord. At some point, the symptoms just disappeared. I hadn't felt God's presence or tingling or heat or anything; the symptoms simply disappeared. I didn't have bronchitis again for at least twenty years.

I once had a vision of a friend of mine. I was in prayer one morning, and the Lord spoke clearly to me that she was planning to kill herself that day. I got up from prayer, went over to her house, and, sure enough, there was a full bottle of a strong narcotic painkiller on the counter that she had retrieved from her husband's doctor bag. She told me that she wanted to use it to end her life. Instead though, I laid hands on her and prayed, and she was delivered of the depressive suicidal spirit that had afflicted her. Within a period of time, she went off all medications and was able to stop seeing the psychiatrist.

There was also the young girl who was miraculously healed of mouth ulcers she contracted from chemotherapy. She had been unable to eat anything for weeks. I prayed for her one afternoon, and that same night she ate some Fritos, those hard, thick, salty corn chips. Wow! I was impressed.

THE DEATH OF MY "FAITH"

There were many more stories, and they crossed my mind as I pondered my past experiences with God's miraculous intervention. But I pulled myself back to the current situation. I said to my family members, "Why don't we gather around her bed and pray?" So we sang a few hymns, and then we began to go around the circle so each family member (except my cousin, who was a skeptic) could pray.

I was both excited and expectant. I just *knew* God was going to heal my aunt. After all, that's why I had come. When my turn came, I obeyed the word I had heard from God, and I laid my hands on her and prayed for her healing. Then I told everyone she was going to be healed.

We waited through the night, but she didn't get any better.

I flew home two days later, and she was still sick.

Within a month, we buried my aunt. She had died of cancer.

I was profoundly shaken. I had been so sure. I had such faith, or at least I felt that I did (and to this day, I believe I did), and I had obeyed God. Either my faith hadn't worked or His Word hadn't.

I entered a season of relentless questioning. Had I heard Him wrong? Was I presumptuous?

I questioned and doubted and struggled. I felt as if I never wanted to put my faith out there again. I didn't want to speak what I believed I had heard the Lord say. I didn't even want to know what He was thinking.

I thought I had heard God before, but I had been wrong. I didn't want to look or feel like a fool again. Somehow I felt like I didn't know God at all now. My faith had died.

REAL FAITH

What I didn't realize is that somehow my faith had become something that I had to work up, think up, and feel up. The burden was all on me. At some point, I began to see that it was not more faith that I needed, but God. I needed God more than ever.

Jessie Penn-Lewis said that it is *dying*, not *doing*, that produces fruit.[1] I had to die to the doing of faith in order to enter into real faith. Believing in God's faith would yield fruit. My eyes had to become focused on Jesus, the author and finisher of my faith. Then things would begin to happen.

Just as the root of all sin is self-reliance, so the root of all faithlessness is also self-reliance. Real faith finds its source in God, not in human beings. This is an eternal truth, but each one of us must discover it for ourselves.

The Israelites, most of them anyway, were just like us. They constantly turned away from God when the going got tough. They tried to find their own solutions. They sought pleasure in earthly delights rather than in God Himself. They preferred other gods, ones that they could touch and see. Since those gods were not real gods at all, in actual fact the people were *self*-reliant. Moses diagnosed the problem:

> Of the Rock who begot you, you are unmindful, and have forgotten the God who fathered you.... He said: "I will hide My face from them, I will see what their end will be, for they are a perverse generation, children in whom is no faith."
>
> —DEUTERONOMY 32:18, 20

Faith is the opposite of self-reliance, and faith is not natural to us. Faith is supernatural; it is of and from God. It is dependent on God.

Faith is revelational, revealed to us by the Holy Spirit. Romans 10:17 says faith comes by hearing and hearing comes by the Word of God. The Greek word for "word" is *rhema*—knowledge that is revealed personally and supernaturally. This is not the same as intellectual knowledge. It is spirit knowledge.

Faith enables us to know and believe in something that is not in existence or seen at the present time:

> Now faith is the assurance (the confirmation, the title deed) of the things [we] hope for, being the proof of things [we] do not see and the conviction of their reality [faith perceiving as real fact what is not revealed to the senses].
>
> —HEBREWS 11:1, AMP

David's Real Faith

Let's return to the story of David and Goliath. As soon as David stepped up to the battlefield, he had faith, and his words reflected his confidence in God's outcome. David's words not only reflected his confidence, but they also created the new outcome. He spoke out of faith, and his words of faith created victory.

David had just had an encounter with God through the prophet Samuel. It had changed the way he talked. His faith-infused words and the resulting outcome of his one small stone formed the grounds on which an entire kingdom was transformed. It's the same with you and me, over and over.

Faith speaks, and then it creates. We are in a day, however, when our words have never been of greater import. That does not change the fact that what I say will create something. What you say will create something. Our faith creates "heaven on earth." It creates solutions, answers, breakthroughs. Our faith is the evidence that we are God's warriors who find our source of victory not in ourselves but in our God. Because of our faith in Him, we become powerful and unbeatable.

It is always God Himself who develops our faith. Often, we encounter seeming defeats along the way. Every warrior must traverse such a journey of faith. Yet if we press on, our faith will become mature. It will arise not out of our minds and our own strength but out of the very heart and voice of God.

We are different as individuals, but we are all alike in our journey, traveling from seeming faith through doubt and unbelief, at times through despair, and always breaking through to something genuine in the end. Eventually, we break through into knowing God in a new way. We stop having faith in ourselves or in a particular outcome and start to have faith in Him who is the source and ground of our lives.

Hope Deferred

Before we reach true faith and true hope, almost always our journey will lead us through a time of serious disappointment and discouragement, a time of having our hope deferred. The proverb is well known: "Hope deferred makes the heart sick..." (Prov. 13:12).

When nothing works out the way you expected it to, your hope is deferred. Something inside you dies. But the second part of that same proverb says, "...but when the desire comes, it is a tree of life."

When something that is dead comes back to life, it has to be a supernatural thing. That's what happened to the dry bones in Ezekiel 37. The army was not only scattered but also in fragments. It was no army at all anymore, just a valley full of dead, bleached, dry bones. Their hope was so deferred that it didn't seem to count anymore.

In order for those bones to become an army again, they had to be resurrected. And in order for them to be resurrected, Ezekiel had to be obedient to God, and he had to speak to those bones—dead, broken bodies that didn't have ears anymore and couldn't really hear for themselves. It was a valley of lost opportunity. The people were all disconnected, even from themselves.

In many ways, this is a picture of the warrior generation that you and I are a part of today. We are scattered, disconnected, dry. We are dead and useless. But words have been going forth. Prayers have been going up. Those heavenly bowls are beginning to tip fresh life over onto us. The warrior generation *will* get back up onto its feet. This whole generation will begin to *generate* again.

Our generation meets the one qualification for new life, and it's simple: *death*. Not very many of us are doing a victory dance. Nothing has worked out the way we thought it should. Instead, we are struggling. Often, God seems so far away.

Are your dreams dead? Have your disappointments sucked the life out of you? Is your youth a thing of the past? Perfect!

Then you are in the right place for a miraculous resurrection. When you have no hope anymore, you are at the end of your rope. Once God makes sure that you are absolutely at the end of your own rope, He will throw you His. But He can't throw you His rope until you let go of your old one.

Why does God let us go through such hard times of having our hope deferred? So we will know beyond a shadow of a doubt that it is the Lord Himself who is doing everything.

We are to be well-trained and well-connected warriors in His army, not independent rebels who pop off a shot every now and then. To the depths of our beings, He wants us to know that He is in charge. He is the sovereign Lord, and we are entirely dependent on Him. He wants us to remember that once we were good and dead, but now we are alive with *His* new life.

We used to be discouraged by the Goliaths around us. We would feel the earth shake with their footsteps, and we would cower in fear. When God came and infused fresh life into us, we rose up like the mighty army generation we were created to be. We became strong and now have the perseverance to stay that way. Now we know what to do with our deferred desires. Our passions rise. We hear His call to battle.

This journey to new life and true faith will look different for each of us. Yet the process and the principles are the same. For you it will be a journey to apprehend faith in one arena, for me in another. Yet through our struggles, at times in despair, our response to God's words enables us to become warriors who can release God's kingdom into the earth around us, in whatever arena of faith we are called to.

SUPERNATURAL EMPOWERING CREATES FAITH

Remember when Samuel poured the oil on David? Something happened to him then. Although in reality he did not sit as king on Saul's throne until many long years later, something happened in the spirit realm when David was anointed—and he knew it.

In a sense, a mantle had been placed on David. That mantle had faith within it. Why do I say that? Because it wasn't a human mantle that David had acquired for himself; it was a mantle of authority that God had placed on him. On his own, David would have been in serious trouble when he encountered the evil spirits in Saul and in Goliath—no matter how good-looking and muscular he was. You can't fight spiritual battles with your human strength.

Jesus said that He would endue us with power to become His witnesses when the Holy Spirit comes upon us (Acts 1:8). In other words, He would grant us and infuse us with miraculous ability to become all that He has called us to be and to do all that He has called us to do. It is an anointing both to be and to do.

If God has called you to be something, to stand in an office or in a calling, then inherent in that call is the ability to stand and walk in it. That means He has given you what you need in order to do what He has called you to do.

David understood the meaning of the anointing and the mantle of authority that God bestowed on him. He knew that it was not for fame and fortune. He knew it would authorize and enable him to be and do whatever God wanted. He had faith in God. Therefore when he went up against an enemy, he already knew that the victory was assured—as long as he remained in the will of God.

God had anointed him to rule over a specific kingdom. That's what a king does. As soon as he was anointed, David started reigning over a kingdom with defined boundaries, even though Saul didn't know it. That meant he could go out there and defeat Goliath. Goliath happened to be standing right in the middle of his field of assignment.

BRINGING FAITH HOME

For most of us, our first field of assignment is our family, the people who are directly related to us. In the context of our families, we learn about love, faith, and responsibility. Living with our families, we begin to understand how living in fellowship creates a kingdom and how this relates to the way that God's kingdom is created as we live in close fellowship with Him.

I asked Inez Harrison to contribute her thoughts on this subject. She has dedicated her energy to defeating the army of Goliaths that have come against the family unit itself. She is a warrior in the arena of family life. She writes:

> The Christian family is a church of sorts, the smallest and most vital cell of the body of Christ. The church community is a family of families. Therefore the family is not only a microcosm of the body of Christ on Earth, but it is also the training ground for the next generation of warriors.
>
> I grew up in a very large family—fifteen children. My father was a pastor. I cannot tell you that I thought of my family as my personal church while I was growing up. In fact, I remember thinking the opposite, that the church was an intrusion into my family. I had heard the phrase "separation of church and state,"

and I determined that when I grew up, there would be a "separation of family and church."

What I didn't know was that my family, and all families, were created and ordained by God to be the building blocks of the church. I also didn't realize how much this fact makes them the target of the enemy.

What does the Bible begin with? A marriage. God created and ordained the first family. His law explicitly protects the family by prohibiting and punishing murder, the dishonoring of parents, adultery, and covetousness, and by forbidding the bearing of false witness against a neighbor and theft (thus protecting the private property ownership of the family). Few biblical teachings are clearer than God's establishment of the monogamous family, with the father as the human authority and his wife as his helper, and with the requirements of love, worship, fellowship, work, obedience, and the godly nurture of children.

What does the Bible end with? Another marriage: a covenantal marriage relationship.

Because of its importance to God's kingdom, the family is being challenged at every turn. The Christian family, especially the role of the father, has been under relentless attack by the forces of darkness. For so many children, there really is no family, at least in the traditional and historically defined sense.

This was my firsthand experience. As I walked through the trenches of disappointment—my own marriage, the death of my husband, life as a single mom raising two sons, wayward children—I clung to my faith that He who had promised would see to it that His promises concerning my family came true.

It was a war I knew I could not win alone. I fully embraced
Joshua 24:15: "As for me and my house, we will serve the Lord."
But I needed weapons in order to come out of the trenches and
win the battle. Like Joshua, I had to wholly set my heart toward
God. I had to learn not to be intimidated by the enemy who
had fierce weapons that could and did ensnare my sons. I had
to learn to listen and follow God's strategic plans, which even
meant moving from one city to another (and in that move, God
captured the hearts of my sons).

Like Joshua, I continuously needed those divine encounters
with the Commander in Chief. Always so independent, I had to
learn to accept the blessings the people of God brought into our
lives. It was an uphill battle of faith.

After years of hard-won victories, God burdened me with a
passion to prepare the next generation to face the battle before
them. Out of this passion in my heart was birthed a nurturing
ministry that puts into the hands of the family the tools and
weapons that can outwit the enemy. My personal church, my
family, and I work together to help other families win the battle
of separation in families and to counter the family-destroying
messages of our culture.

Winning this battle, one family at a time, will affect the
present-day situation, and it will create a God-centered future
for generations to come.

THE POWER OF FAITH WORDS

Whether it's in the context of a family, a ministry, a business, or a
church, faith must be spoken and acted on. "Faith without works is
dead" (James 2:20, 26). Faith speaks both through words and through
actions.

Because David believed God, he went up against Goliath. He acted. In the process of acting, he spoke aloud words of faith. Look at David's first words to the men on the battlefield: "For who is this uncircumcised Philistine, that he should defy the armies of the living God?" (1 Sam. 17:26).

David then went before Saul and said more words. Here is faith speaking: "Let no man's heart fail because of him; your servant will go and fight with this Philistine" (v. 32). In other words, David was saying, "I'm not just boasting. My words arise out of my unshakable trust in God. I will go out and fight him."

There is a progression here. First, David asked a question of the soldiers who were standing by. He spoke to ordinary people. Then he moved to speak to the king, the one in authority, the one with legal right in the matter, to let him know that he was up to the task.

David would fight the Philistine. He went before Goliath himself, addressing Goliath head-on, face-to-face, as he made a confession of his faith. Faith spoke through David.

Not only did David address Goliath to tell him he was going to fight him, but he also informed him that he would overcome him. "Listen to me, Goliath! You're about to become 'dead meat'!" (See 1 Samuel 17:46.) The clincher is David's declaration that it was not to come through his own might but through the might of the Lord. Specifically, "I come to you in the name of the Lord of hosts, the God of the armies of Israel, whom you have defied" (v. 45).

David was declaring his legal right to stand before Goliath and to slay him. Further, he was declaring that it was not his idea but God's idea.

God was David's source. What was his purpose? To kill Goliath so that he could demonstrate and declare that there was a God in Israel. It was to make a visible display before all the people of Israel, as well as the Philistines, that God was in control and that no enemy is ever too hard for Him.

It was fitting for this triumph to become a public spectacle. Paul depicted it when he wrote, "Having disarmed principalities and powers, He [Christ] made a public spectacle of them, triumphing over them in it" (Col. 2:15).

In those days, an invading army would make a public display of their victory. One of the ways they would do it was by parading through the city streets and the central square dragging a defeated king's body behind a chariot so that the populace could see that he had been over-taken, killed, and altogether defeated. Another way was to display a defeated leader's body or his head on the city wall.

After Goliath was slain before the eyes of the troops of Philistine and Israel, he was decapitated by David so that his head could be displayed in Jerusalem. (See 1 Samuel 17:54.) With their own eyes, everyone could see the victory of Israel over the Philistines.

So it is today. When God speaks to us to accomplish something, we then declare it publicly at the right time. If what we do is from God, the next thing that occurs is a public manifestation of the results.

Later in this book, I tell the story of our part in the Malice Green trial in Detroit, Michigan. In a public meeting, we did exactly what God told us to do, which was to repent. We declared aloud that God would intervene because of this action. And He did. On the front page of *USA Today*, the headlines read something like this: "Riot Averted in Detroit."[2] A public spectacle was made of the devil's intended activities.

HOW FORCIBLE ARE RIGHT WORDS

In his book *Authority in Prayer,* Dutch Sheets begins a chapter by quoting from the book of Job: "How forcible are right words!" (Job 6:25, KJV). He points out that:

- Wars are started with words.
- Love is communicated through words.
- Instruction and education are shared by words.
- Deception and confusion are propagated by words.
- Kingdoms are built by words.
- People are controlled by words.
- Lives are shattered and healed through words.
- Worlds are created by words—the earth was, and so is our personal world.[3]

Just as words have the power to destroy a person's life, right words have the power to restore life. Faith words have supernatural clout. When was the last time you spoke world-altering words that came straight from your God-born faith?

As one of the Davidic people of this warrior generation, have you moved into your role of *declaration?* There is power in the right words spoken at the right time.

When David was standing in the Valley of Elah, he was standing in the gap. He was standing in the breach where communion had been broken because of fear. He did not kneel down there and pray silently, petitioning God for strength and victory. No, he kept standing up and moved right into position before Goliath. He raised his voice and used words born of faith to declare the end from the beginning.

That's what we should do too. As intercessors, we stand in the gap between man and God. We stand in the place where the battle is raging. We stand there on God's behalf, representing His heart toward the people, toward the human systems, toward the kingdom that is under attack. We boldly go up against the enemy with confidence and full authority, speaking directly to the Goliath in control, declaring what is and what will be.

As a giant, Goliath symbolically represents systems, fields, kingdoms, arenas of power, and authority. When a Goliath comes down, whole nations are set free. We are living in a time when armies of Davids like you and me have been prepared to stand in the face of the giants of society. Through our faith declarations and strategically equipped actions, we are being positioned to defeat those systems and make a public spectacle of them.

Some of us are in action right now. Some of us are being prepared for the next battle. As we walk closely with God, we are being raised up with resurrection life, and we can expect our words to take on new authority. Because we know who is in charge, we can disregard the risks of the battlefield. Our lives are not our own; in fact, we have died to our old lives altogether.

> For we who live are constantly [experiencing] being handed over to death for Jesus' sake, that the resurrection life of Jesus also may be evidenced through our flesh which is liable to death. Thus death is actively at work in us, but [it is in order that our] life [may be actively at work] in you. Yet we have the same spirit of faith as he had who wrote, I have believed, and therefore have I spoken. We too believe, and therefore we speak.
>
> —2 CORINTHIANS 4:11–13, AMP

Like Paul in this passage, we continually run into the end of our own resources—physically, emotionally, mentally, and spiritually. Yet we also constantly run into the life of God, and God's resources cause us to have great faith and ability.

Our faith arises from the death side of the Cross, where we have surrendered everything to God and where we have died to self-reliance. With God as the source of our strength, faith, and life, we qualify to bring heaven to Earth with all of its creativity and glory, supernatural solutions and victories.

AS FAITH SPEAKS, FAITH CREATES

So when we express our faith aloud in words, our faith swings into action. When faith speaks, watch out because entire systems will begin to fall and new ones will arise to replace them. When Davids speak, they release their "one small stone" into the atmosphere, some simple strategy that God has given them to defeat the enemy. The defeat is created through their words. The strategy that was formulated in heaven is released, and the freedom from bondage is released along with it.

Scripture says the words of the wise are like "goads" or nails, fastened into place by those who are the masters of the words (Eccles. 12:11). When we release our faith-originated, wise words, they serve as goads—prodding, motivating, stirring, driving somebody to take action. Structures and systems that seemed to be immovable are taken down. The words finish things off and secure the territory for the kingdom of God. A new order of things comes into being.

When faith speaks, situations are turned around, people are moved forward, and change occurs. Most of all, God is glorified. With Him, heaven comes to Earth.

8

The Heart of the Battle

I READ AN ARTICLE ABOUT A CHRISTIAN BUSINESSMAN WHO was a shaker and a mover, a thinker and a doer. He ran a multinational corporation, and he moved mega dollars. You could say that he was a "corporate warrior," one who guarded a corporate kingdom and who made sure that it flourished and stayed on the cutting edge. Yet until he was in his forties, he reported that he had been oblivious to his own feelings—he didn't have any idea how important it was to pay attention to what they were telling him.

He came to the end of himself and burned out. He ran into a wall. He crashed. As a result, he learned something about himself, and that is what the article was about. Because of his experience, he discovered that he had a *heart*. And he learned how important his heart is.

Why did he burn out? Because he had guarded his corporation, but he had not guarded his own heart—he had abandoned it. He didn't even know that his heart was the most critical faculty he possessed. He didn't know it was the key to his personhood and therefore his key to knowing where he was in any battle.

People who can't feel can't locate themselves.

Finding out about his heart also meant that the businessman discovered his capacity to be vulnerable. Vulnerability is both an asset and a liability, of course. But warriors (that includes corporate warriors) need to be able to feel, to be in touch with their feelings, to "have a heart," and to know their hearts.

Your Heart Is Central to Successful Warfare

Your heart provides clues for you as to what you are up against. If you can't find your heart, you are handicapped. You won't be able to locate your passion, your motivational core, your love. You won't understand what makes you mad and what makes you glad.

Consequently, you will be unable to discern if you are discouraged, grieved, angry, happy, joyful, or anything else. To a degree, you will be robotic. If you notice that you have feelings, you will tend to bury them so you can try to ignore them, because to you, your feelings seem like things that get in the way of your productivity, success, and victory.

If you cannot find your heart, not only will you not be able to pay attention to its messages, but also you won't know how to watch over it and guard it. You won't be alert to danger or threats.

Furthermore, you will not be able to connect with others except on an intellectual level. You won't be able to connect with their hearts if you can't even find your own. You won't be able to empathize with others except on a superficial level. You won't be able to "get into their skin." This means that you will be lonely when the crowd leaves, which will make you bury yourself in more "doing." You will search for your identity and significance through what you *do* rather than who you *are*, and ultimately you will lose your way in the battle of life.

To be effective and whole, you need to be able to develop and sustain relationships with other people and with God. You need to possess clarity of personal identity.

If you know and understand your heart, you can talk and walk with

God. You can be in a living heart-to-heart relationship with a real God who is your Father and who will help you to discern the path ahead of you. By speaking to your heart, He can reveal strategies to you and help you break through to new levels of victory. God cares about you. He wants you to succeed. He loves you.

BURIED EMOTIONS

As a child, I learned to suppress my heart. In my family, we somehow picked up the idea that it was a sin to express emotions. Either we had feelings and hid them, or we kept feelings so shut down that we didn't even recognize them.

We were a typical evangelical family, a good family in many ways. We did things together and loved each other. But we did not know how to work through disagreements or problems.

Any time there was a disagreement or any negative feelings expressed, everyone scattered like roaches when the lights are turned on. To this day, I do not know how those feelings ever got resolved. I suppose we just buried our emotions, or we learned to at least suppress the expression of our feelings.

As a result, by the time I became an adult, I was blind as a bat when it came to my heart and emotions. I could not recognize when I was challenged relationally or emotionally. I did not know what to do when I came under attack. I would just suddenly become aware of this tangled ball of feelings, and I'd run for cover. And I wouldn't come out until somehow those feelings dissolved.

This created a situation in which (unbeknownst to me) the enemy had a legal right to my heart and emotions. Why? Because I could not identify them. I did not know where they were coming from or how to deal with them.

As a result, I could not rule over my own spirit because my emotions were already in control. They would suddenly erupt like a volcano and take me over by surprise. Or sometimes it would appear to other people that I was having different feelings than what I was really having.

I will never forget one incident that happened late at night in a grocery store. I was bone tired and waiting in a checkout line at about 10:30 p.m. Suddenly a woman came along and pushed her cart into the line, right in front of me.

I was so exhausted that I didn't even care. I looked at the woman with what I thought was a pitiful expression because I felt like I would drop dead right then out of exhaustion. She looked back at me and said, "What are you so mad about?"

I thought to myself, "Well, you did just butt into the line in front of me!" But I was too exhausted to protest. However, I remembered years ago how my husband had at times asked me what I was angry about when I did not feel angry at all. It had always puzzled me and bothered me. I realized that when I was exceptionally tired, I must have gotten a look on my face that my husband and others interpreted as anger.

From that day on, I learned to notify people when I was in that state of exhaustion. "I might look mad, but I'm not," I began to tell everyone. "I'm just exhausted." Just doing that has prevented a lot of misunderstandings from happening.

Someone had to point out what my face looked like before I could identify my true feelings. I had to come to know myself in a new way.

IGNORANCE OPENS A DOOR TO THE ENEMY

Our ignorance about our feelings does not keep us from being wounded in the battle of life. In fact, our ignorance opens a door to wounds.

Satan comes through that door of ignorance and gains an advantage over us simply because we don't stop him.

This is a biblical idea. Paul, writing about the importance of forgiveness, advised believers to forgive in order "to keep Satan from getting the advantage over us; for we are not ignorant of his wiles and intentions" (2 Cor. 2:11, AMP).

In the Greek, the word *advantage* means "to gain a position of control," and *ignorance* means "to lack information or understanding." In other words, to keep the devil from controlling our thoughts and behavior, we must endeavor to know and understand ourselves to the best of our ability.

Personally, I recommend that people gain knowledge about themselves by taking profiles or evaluations to help them understand their personalities, their leadership abilities, their relational strengths and weaknesses, and other aspects of their personal makeup.

Often other people can see things from a different perspective than I can. So I also make it a priority in my life to cultivate personal friendships with people with whom I can share my heart struggles, people to whom I give the right to speak into my life. My friends help me gain understanding and wisdom about myself. The more I am self-aware, the less I can be taken by surprise. "In a multitude of counselors there is safety" (Prov. 24:6).

Of course, there is a sense in which none of us will ever totally know ourselves. The prophet Jeremiah wrote, "The heart is deceitful above all things, and desperately wicked; who can know it?" (Jer. 17:9). But that doesn't mean that we shouldn't try.

God does not intend for us to be continually taken off guard through our ignorance. Paul wrote in Philippians 3:15 that if there is any way we are unaware of what is in our minds and hearts, God will make it

clear to us. If we take the whole counsel of God, we find an abundance
of heart-related advice:

> Above all else, guard your heart, for it is the wellspring of life.
>
> —Proverbs 4:23, niv

> Wisdom rests in the heart of him who has understanding.
>
> —Proverbs 14:33

> The heart of him who has understanding seeks knowledge, but
> the mouth of fools feeds on foolishness.
>
> —Proverbs 15:14

> The heart of the righteous studies how to answer, but the mouth
> of the wicked pours forth evil.
>
> —Proverbs 15:28

> The heart of the wise teaches his mouth, and adds learning to
> his lips.
>
> —Proverbs 16:23

> My son, if your heart is wise, my heart will rejoice—indeed, I
> myself; yes, my inmost being will rejoice when your lips speak
> right things.
>
> —Proverbs 23:15–16

> Therefore we do not lose heart. Though outwardly we are
> wasting away, yet inwardly we are being renewed day by day.
>
> —2 Corinthians 4:16, niv

To be successful as a warrior, I had to follow all this advice and learn
to identify my heart and my emotions. So do you. We have to learn

where the assaults are coming from and how they affect us inside as well as what action we need to take to get back on our feet emotionally when something knocks us down.

We *must* know our hearts.

BODY, SOUL, AND SPIRIT

To help us know our hearts, we need to understand the difference between our bodies, our souls, and our spirits. I asked Jay Pike, who was part of the pastoral team at my church, to write something about this.

> When you look in the mirror, the thing you see there is not really you. It is really just your house, the tent that the real you lives in. Inside that tent, you find your soul and your spirit. Your soul includes your mind, your will, and your emotions.
>
> Your soul consists of your thoughts, decisions, and feelings. It's the part of you that makes you unique; it gives you your personality. Your soul expresses who you are to others—outgoing or shy, fast paced or laid back, funny or serious. Your soul is the same as your "heart."
>
> Your spirit is the innermost part of you. It is the "real you." Your spirit is the part of you that God dwells in. Until you came to know Christ, the real you was "dead in trespasses and sin" (Eph. 2:1). It comes alive when you are born again.
>
> The great truth of the gospel is not that Jesus died to improve our current life but that He died so we could live an entirely new life. Understanding that your body and soul are given to you at natural birth, but your spirit is made alive when you are spiritually born, is paramount to living the life God has designed for you.

When you accept Christ, you enter an entirely new realm of possibilities. That's why for a Christian, it doesn't matter if anyone in your family ever graduated from college, ever traveled the world, ever started a business, or ever owned a home. When you choose to follow Christ, your life ceases to be limited by your genes and your experiences. Now it is limited only by God's wonderful design for you.

Paul describes your new life in Ephesians 3:20 by saying that it is "exceedingly abundantly above all that we ask or think." That's the life of a warrior—a life without limits.

We get our bodies from our genes we inherit from our parents and grandparents. (That can either be a blessing, or not much of a blessing!) Our souls are shaped largely by our past experiences. The way we think, feel, and make decisions is greatly impacted by the things we've been through. But our spirits come from and are shaped by God.

It is crucial to understand that the life God has designed for you can be found only in the dimensions of your spirit man. Everyone on earth has access to his or her body and soul, but only believers have full access to the spiritual dimensions of their lives.

Our bodies live by sensation, our souls live by information, but our spirits live by something entirely different. Jesus said that "Man does not live on bread alone, but on every word that comes from the mouth of God" (Matt. 4:4, NIV). What He is saying is that our spirit man does not live by sensation or information but by *revelation*.

If you can carry out your life through simple sensation (what feels right) and information (what you know), then you are living life below the realm of God's design. Whereas sensation and information come from the outside in, through our natural senses, revelation comes from the inside out, through our spiritual senses and ability to hear words that come from the mouth of God.

When God speaks to us, He does not speak to our bodies or minds. He speaks to our spirits. If we live life only by information and sensation, we can live our whole Christian lives and never touch God's design for our lives! Warriors are people who commit to live not by their past experiences or the limitations of their genetics, but they live for the future God has designed for them. The warrior life that God is calling you to live demands that you hear from Him in your spirit man.

Every time we are faced with a decision, the issue of spirit, soul, and body is played out; a vote is held inside the councils of your being. Your body votes for what feels good now. Your spirit votes for what is best for your future and what will align you with God's design for your life. And your soul is caught in the middle.

Paul tells us that spirit and the flesh "are contrary to one another" (Gal. 5:17). Our spirits move in one direction and our bodies move in another. Our soul, which includes our will or decision-making ability, casts the deciding vote.

Your soul (your heart) will follow whichever part of you exerts the most influence over it at any given time. If your body is stronger, then bye-bye, spirit man. But if your spirit is the strongest part of you, your body will quietly submit to your Spirit-controlled soul and align with God's future for your life.

WHAT IS THE HEART?

One of the synonyms for heart is "center." Other words for center are *core, nucleus, hub, central point, central part, focal point.* That gives us something to think about!

What else can we say about our heart of hearts? (We're not talking about the physical, blood-pumping organ in your chest.) Here are some dictionary-based observations:

- Your heart is the basis, source, and center of your emotional life, the place where your deepest and sincerest feelings are located and where you are the most vulnerable to pain.

- Your heart is the core of your character. It is where compassion comes from, and it is the place from which humane and altruistic feelings emerge. It is your center of affection; warmth, love, and admiration for others come from your heart.

- Your heart is where your capacity for courage and determination arise from, the place where you develop "a heart for" something.

- A heart is the most essential part of something, its distinctive, significant, and characteristic center, as in the expression, "the heart of the matter."

- Your heart is linked with your core feelings such as devotion, attitudes, and desires. When I "take something to heart," I take it seriously. Something has the capacity to touch me, to upset me, to affect my emotions, to motivate me. When I do something "with my whole heart," I do it completely and willingly. If I "take heart," I become more encouraged and confident.

Did you know that your heart is under siege? You must watch over and guard your heart because there is a war over it. Proverbs 4:23 in the Amplified Bible stresses the watchman aspect, stating, "Keep and guard [Hebrew *shamar*, "to keep, to guard, to watch over"] your heart with all vigilance and above all that you guard, for out of it flow the springs of life."

If the enemy can capture your heart, he can shut down the life that flows out of you. By capturing your heart, your core, he can control you. He has you!

In a previous chapter I quoted, "Hope deferred makes the heart sick" (Prov. 13:12). It's the same as with our physical hearts. Our hearts make the blood flow to all parts of our bodies. If a person's heart fails, then that person becomes sick, weak, anemic, bloodless, and lacking in nourishment. When breathless, he can't breathe because fluid accumulates in his lungs. If the heart fails, the whole body will fail; each organ will begin to shut down and die.

Not long ago I visited a friend of mine. Her heart had failed and fluid had backed up in her lungs. I watched as she struggled to breathe. Additionally, she couldn't talk because every time she talked, she coughed. She couldn't walk, because any exercise made her breathless. Her color had become a strange dusky gray-blue. She was becoming lifeless. Her eyes had stopped dancing. She lay there on the bed, struggling for every breath, all because her heart had failed.

That is a picture of you or me spiritually and emotionally when our heart, soul, and spirit fail.

CAPTURED BY UNRESOLVED ASSAULTS

In battle, the enemy looks for our weaknesses and our unresolved wounds. Then he plays off them. All of a sudden, thoughts and feelings erupt that we thought we were over and done with.

When we are caught in the enemy's crossfire, unresolved pain and hurt from childhood issues will erupt. Anything we have not worked through will usually come to the surface in the midst of such a time, even if it seems to have nothing to do with the current situation. The enemy's assaults rampage on and keep us from obtaining the victory of our inheritance in Christ.

What this means is that you are much more vulnerable in battle if you carry unhealed wounds in your heart. As you work to identify and deal with wounded places in your life, consider the following list of possibilities:

1. Past sins against you over which you had no control (This includes any kind of abuse, betrayal, etc.)

2. Past sins you knowingly committed

3. Generational iniquities that have found a place in you. Iniquities are family weaknesses, tendencies to sin in certain areas. Remember how Abraham lied, and then his son Isaac lied? That is an example of a generational iniquity. Generational iniquities often are accompanied by familial spirits, spirits that follow a family bloodline, waiting for an opportune time to attack.

4. Familiar spirits or demonic entities that know your weaknesses and that come to visit you at the most inopportune times

5. Marital dissatisfaction or discord that opens you up to wrong relationships or sinful actions

As you may know, one of the names of Satan is Beelzebub, which means "lord of the flies." Flies are attracted to garbage. In fact, flies lay their eggs in garbage, and soon the garbage can is filled with their larvae. Garbage is their garden of multiplication; they exponentially multiply in it.

So it is in our hearts. If we have "garbage" in our hearts—past hurts, unhealed wounds, unresolved issues—our hearts become the breeding ground for the enemy forces.

By definition and by assignment, warriors are in the midst of war. They are on a battlefield. On every battlefield is an enemy who is seeking to gain the position of advantage. An enemy does not care how the advantage is won. He simply fights for it and seizes it the moment it becomes available.

THE UNSEEN WAR

So often, you and I forget that we are on a battlefield because the war is an unseen one.[1]

Things are not as they seem to be. Paul said that he was praying for the Ephesians that the eyes of their understanding would be enlightened (Eph. 1:18). He was saying, in other words, "Let them see what's behind the things they see, because it is very real even though it is unseen." Unseen enemies are just as real as the ones we can see. We are in a battle far more than we recognize. Consider this familiar passage:

> Wake up from your sleep, climb out of your coffins; Christ will show you the light! So watch your step. Use your head. Make the most of every chance you get. These are desperate times!

Don't live carelessly, unthinkingly. Make sure you understand
what the Master wants.

—EPHESIANS 5:15–17, THE MESSAGE

We are often fooled and deceived about the real truth. It doesn't
matter how "good" we are. Even Daniel could not see that there was an
invisible demonic prince, the prince of Persia, who was holding back
the answer to his prayers. (See Daniel 10:20.)

We are a world at war. War is currently being waged over every
believer, over the church, and over nations. There is war over prophets,
apostles, and everything new in the establishment and advancement of
the kingdom of God on the earth. The enemy's goal in this war is to
keep us from breaking through to the redemptive purposes and destiny
of God.

You and I have crucial roles to play in this war. To find our models,
we can look to others who have gone before us. They too warred and
won, breaking through discouragement and darkness to bring in a
little more of God's kingdom. Look at the apostle Paul. Look at Moses,
Joshua, David, Esther, Deborah, Anna, Peter, and countless others in
the Bible. Look at Frodo and Sam in *The Lord of the Rings*. Do you
see what a crucial role each of them had to play? Look at Joan of Arc,
an ordinary farm girl who ended up leading armies into war. Look at
Mother Teresa, another ordinary woman whose name is now a house-
hold word. (Recently it was revealed that she possessed major doubts
about her relationship with God for over fifty years.[2] She was in a war
the whole time.)

What we struggle with the most is our significance in the war. We
ask ourselves, "Am I really making a difference? Am I at all important
to God in this effort?" If we really understand the glory that God wants

to reveal in and through each of us, knowing in the core of our hearts that it is true, everything will change, and the enemy's power will be diminished and neutralized.

DAVID, THE HEART MAN

David, the warrior king, was a "heart man." He was a man of passion who was after God's heart. He was both a lover and a warrior because of the intensity of his heart's passion.

Remember that the name David means "to boil hot." David was intense. Everything about him came from his heart of passion, including his sin. His heart was both his strength and his downfall. He looked at Bathsheba, and his passion caused him to sin. He not only committed adultery, but he also ordered the murder of Bathsheba's husband, Uriah, who had been one of his most faithful and loyal leaders. (See 2 Samuel 11–12.)

Earlier in David's career, we see the battle over his heart at Ziklag. (See 1 Samuel 30.) The Amalekites had destroyed the city and had taken captive all of the women and children. Those people included David's family as well as the families of his army. When David and his men discovered what had happened, they were stunned and dumbstruck, then grief-stricken and enraged. The men wailed. Then they turned on David. They wanted to kill him to retaliate for their losses.

David's heart was torn in two. He too was heartsick and brokenhearted because of the devastation. He cared about his own family, and he cared about the families of his men. He was at war within and without—with himself and with the other men. However, "David strengthened himself in the Lord his God" (1 Sam. 30:6). He found a place in God where he could be encouraged. Who knows what would have happened otherwise? It could have been the end of David.

So you see that on top of the great military defeat at Ziklag, the enemy was after David's heart by exploiting the situation, heaping on discouragement, despair, sin, desperation, and hopelessness. The enemy knew that if he could control David's heart, he could control his life.

But the tide of the battle turned. Led by David, the troops regained their wives and children and goods, and he regained their favor. It had been a major battle of the heart.

DO NOT LOSE HEART

"Therefore we do not lose heart" (2 Cor. 4:16). Paul says something significant here. In the midst of our contending for the faith, in the effort to break through to victory in our areas of assignment, there is the potential for becoming wounded in heart and for losing heart. There is the potential for floundering in discouragement and therefore in defeat. When we are in a battle, the enemy will attempt to defeat us in any possible way.

But thanks be to God, we do not lose the battle over our hearts. The Amplified Bible uses "discouraged" instead of "losing heart," and it goes on to describe such battles as momentary afflictions on the path of glory:

> Therefore we do not become *discouraged (utterly spiritless,*
> *exhausted, and wearied out through fear)*. Though our outer
> man is [progressively] decaying and wasting away, yet our inner
> self is being [progressively] renewed day after day. For our light,
> momentary affliction (this slight distress of the passing hour)
> is ever more and more abundantly preparing and producing
> and achieving for us an everlasting weight of glory [beyond all
> measure, excessively surpassing all comparisons and all calcu-
> lations, a vast and transcendent glory and blessedness never to

cease!], since we consider and look not to the things that are seen but to the things that are unseen; for the things that are visible are temporal (brief and fleeting), but the things that are invisible are deathless and everlasting.

—2 CORINTHIANS 4:16–18, AMP, EMPHASIS ADDED

Remember what Paul said: do not become discouraged; do not lose heart. As you and I engage in warfare, and as we continue to fight for a cause, warring for a field, a kingdom that God wants to deliver into our hands, there will come a time when the enemy will assault our hearts. He will assault them unrelentingly. He will use anything—our seeming lack of success or previous wounds from the battle—to assault us with every kind of negative emotion. He will bury us in disappointment, rage, anger, bitterness, hopelessness, despair, unforgiveness, rejection, and abandonment. He will allow personal attacks that send us reeling, and he will aggravate relationship disagreements, breaches, and betrayals.

The enemy will generate in us a desire to quit, to get out, to stop, and to give up. He will use sickness, everything from persistent minor physical problems to serious, life-threatening illnesses. He will use financial setbacks, marital conflicts, family problems, and just about anything stressful that you can think of. He wants to stop you. He wants to wound you. He wants to wipe you out.

That's why Paul cries out, "Do not lose heart!" If you lose heart, for whatever reason, you will give up. A heart that is broken cannot function. Whatever wounds and breaks your heart will undermine your strength, cripple you, and weaken you to the point that you allow the enemy to take territory away from you.

Conflict, trouble, pressure, and the stress of seemingly unsolvable problems can make us crazy. We become vulnerable, and the enemy can catch us off guard. We become fearful and anxious and even panicked, all of which make us unable to connect with God through faith.

Without faith, we cannot access the strategies of heaven, and we cannot break through hindrances.

The Israelites constantly fought an inner battle regarding their trust in God and His promises. They lost heart. They gave in to doubt and unbelief. They abandoned faith. Then they believed an evil report. They declared with their lips that what God had said was possible was, in fact, impossible. They spoke out of their doubting, fearful hearts. The result was that their doubt and unbelief kept them from obtaining the promises of God.

Proverbs 23:7 says as a man "thinks in his heart, so is he." We are what we think in our hearts. Jesus said that it is out of the abundance of the heart that the mouth speaks (Matt. 12:34; Luke 6:45). In other words, our speech gives our hearts away.

Look what happened with the Israelites. Then look at your own heart. What are you saying, declaring, speaking, shouting, or murmuring? As you think in your heart, you will speak. As you speak, you declare the outcome of the battle that rages within and around you. What is in your heart? That is what you are. As Proverbs 27:19 states, "As in water face reflects face, so a man's heart reveals the man."

This is why we must both know and guard our hearts! Our hearts are at the heart of the battle every time.

9

The Time for Revolution

J ESUS WAS A REVOLUTIONARY. HE WAS THE ONE to whom John
the Baptist, the forerunner, had been pointing. He was the One
through whom the kingdom of God would be released into the
earth. He was the new thing. He was revolution in person, the force
that would ultimately turn the world upside down.

Revolution was and is in the heart, mind, and spirit of the man Jesus,
and since we have been called to follow Him, we have also been called
to join Him on the battlefield. Jesus was a revolutionary from the beginning, and He is still empowering His followers to be co-revolutionaries
with Him today.

In the Book of Revelation, what is the picture of Jesus but a military
one? He is a picture of a true revolutionary:

> After that I saw heaven opened, and behold, a white horse
> [appeared]! The One Who was riding it is called Faithful
> (Trustworthy, Loyal, Incorruptible, Steady) and True, and He
> passes judgment and wages war in righteousness (holiness,
> justice, and uprightness). His eyes [blaze] like a flame of fire,
> and on His head are many kingly crowns (diadems); and He has
> a title (name) inscribed which He alone knows or can under-
> stand. He is dressed in a robe dyed by dipping in blood, and the
> title by which He is called is The Word of God. And the troops

of heaven, clothed in fine linen, dazzling and clean, followed Him on white horses. From His mouth goes forth a sharp sword with which He can smite (afflict, strike) the nations; and He will shepherd and control them with a staff (scepter, rod) of iron. He will tread the winepress of the fierceness of the wrath and indignation of God the All-Ruler (the Almighty, the Omnipotent).

—REVELATION 19:11–15, AMP

There we see Him in all His glory—the warrior King, Jesus.

JESUS MAKES US REVOLUTIONARIES

On the Day of Pentecost, the Spirit of Jesus—with revolutionary implications—was poured out on those who were waiting in the Upper Room. This caused a phenomenal reaction. The disciples ran out into the streets acting as if they were drunk. They uttered words in languages that they themselves did not know, although the people who were in the city streets that day understood them.

Most of the people in the streets had come to Jerusalem from many different nations to celebrate the Feast of Weeks, and suddenly they were hearing the good news proclaimed in their own languages. The people were dumbfounded. Who were these drunks? The words kept pouring out of their mouths, but anyone could tell from looking at them that they were ordinary Jews, whose appearance did not match the languages they were speaking.

Jesus had stated that this outpouring would be for the purpose of giving His followers power to be effective witnesses. He could also have said it would create a revolution, because that is what happened. From that day forward, the greatest ever grassroots movement of revival and awakening began to spread like wildfire. Cities were changed; nations were changed. Single individuals were able to bring the gospel to entire nations. (Remember how Philip evangelized the Ethiopian eunuch, who returned to Ethiopia and started a revival in Africa?)

People returned to their homes after the Day of Pentecost, and they brought the message with them. The city of Jerusalem was changed forever because so many of its residents were converted.

Later, Paul went to Ephesus, preached the gospel in a city that had been controlled by the goddess Diana, and introduced a transformation that was not only religious but also governmental, social, and educational as well. This spiritual Jesus revolution kept on going. It rolled like an endless tidal wave across the Middle East, Africa, and Europe, then to the rest of the civilized world. We're still riding that wave today.

Have you been swept up in the wave of God? Let's consider what it means to be a revolutionary warrior.

REVOLUTION MEANS REVOLVE

Look at the word *revolution*. It carries the meaning of when something revolves, it rotates; it turns around in a circle. A revolution revolves. It can turn a nation around. The gospel message has turned nations around repeatedly (and usually without bloodshed).

In our day, I don't think anyone would argue with the fact that the United States of America needs to be turned around. The times are becoming more and more desperate. Political factions squabble and squander enormous amounts of time and money, while the economy seems to teeter on the verge of collapse. The debt load has never been greater. Division, trouble, and disenchantment seem to be the words of the day—even within the church, which is filled with disgruntled believers. With a passion, the world at large hates the United States and all it stands for.

To initiate the release of a new revolutionary cycle, Lou Engle led the nation in a day of prayer and fasting in the summer of 2007, in Nashville, Tennessee. He wanted to make it possible for the United States of America to turn around.

Perhaps you were there.

Known as "TheCall," this was a call to all generations, but especially to the current generation of young people, to take the cycle that had started forty years earlier in 1967, the hippie revolution, and turn it into a God revolution. Lou proclaimed, "Let's turn this thing!" and eighty thousand people, young and old, cried out to God for a spiritual revolution in the nation. They worshiped, prayed, interceded, sought forgiveness, declared, and cried out in a radical, fervent, intense unity of faith and action.

As part of the turnaround, Dutch Sheets led the people in a time of "divorcing Baal" and coming into a new covenantal marriage relationship with God Himself. He and the others who prayed were laying the foundation for a new, sweeping, spiritual revolution across this nation. Through fervent prayer and intercession for spiritual awakening like this, people are paving the way for it to happen.

REVOLUTION MEANS SOCIAL CHANGE

Any large, fundamental social change is the same as what some people in the church are calling a "transformation." In Webster's dictionary, one of the definitions of *revolution* is, in fact, transformation. It means change, reform, alteration, conversion, innovation, modernization, development, and the like.

Social transformation is fundamental to revolution. Every revolution, whether it occurs with a formal declaration of war or not, brings social change with it. Think of revolutions you have heard about and the social changes they have accomplished. The hippie revolution over-turned the established morals of the United States within a span of a few decades. The Industrial Revolution transformed the Western world from an agrarian, rural society to an urbanized, mechanized one.

The Revolutionary War in the colonies that had come out of Great Britain and had established the New World created the United States of America and initiated rapid territorial expansion across the North American continent. The Cultural Revolution in China transformed the social fabric of that nation, effecting sweeping reforms that paved the way for China to become what it is today, a mixture of capitalism and communism.

In a positive way, true spiritual revivals almost always revolutionize a society for the good. Think about the great revivals of Europe and the United States. In the mid-1800s, the country of England had slipped into abject degradation. Prostitution was rampant. The British Parliament had lowered the age at which a man could have sex with a girl to a mere thirteen years to make it legal for their own members (as well as other leading members of society) to continue the practice. But a spiritual revival arose in response, in part motivated by William and Catherine Booth (founders of The Salvation Army), releasing the presence and power of God to change not only individuals but also the entire social system. In fact, William Booth wrote a brilliant strategy for the rehabili-tation of the entire nation called *In Darkest England and the Way Out*.[1]

Over a hundred years earlier, there were approximately two hundred fifty thousand people living in New England. The Holy Spirit used Jonathan Edwards to spearhead what is now known as the Great Awak-ening, when fifty thousand of these people were saved. This sweeping move of God did not stop in the hearts of individual people; it extended to change society itself, including education and government.[2]

149

The apostle Paul talks about how spiritual renewal creates transformation in the mind. He exhorts his readers:

> Do not be conformed to this world, but be transformed by the renewing of your mind, that you may prove what is that good and acceptable and perfect will of God.
>
> —ROMANS 12:2

The word *transformed* here means to be changed to the extent that our very form, shape, and structure are different. The same word is used to speak of how a caterpillar turns into a butterfly. That is the kind of radical transformation we can expect to see in any society that God's Spirit touches.

REVOLUTION MEANS REVOLT

A revolution is a revolt. In other words, it is a rebellion, an uprising, an upheaval, an insurgency, an insurrection, a mutiny, or even a riot.

Societies experience revolution when leaders arise from the ranks of young, zealous idealists. Karl Marx was such a leader. The upheaval at China's Tiananmen Square in 1989 was another such uprising.

This aspect of the meaning of revolution involves the use of violence to effect a transfer of political rights. While this may seem unattractive or inappropriate to us as Christians, it shouldn't seem like a foreign concept if we remember a few key passages of Scripture. For instance, remember the words of Jesus:

> From the days of John the Baptist until now the kingdom of heaven suffers violence, and the violent take it by force.
>
> —MATTHEW 11:12

The Time for Revolution

You and I are called to rise up and lead a rebellion over the enemy, Satan, and all of his power and political influence. Because of Jesus, we are enabled to rise up with powerful new life:

> By this the love of God was manifested in us, that God has sent His only begotten Son into the world so that we might live through Him.
>
> —1 JOHN 4:9, NAS

We become participants in an uprising that overturns the power of the enemy. We are part of a holy insurgency, an insurrection, a mutiny on board Satan's ship. We will riot, if that's what it takes, in order to undo his controlling interests.

The apostle John said that the reason Jesus came into the world was to "undo (destroy, loosen, and dissolve) the works the devil [has done]" (1 John 3:8, AMP). What was that but a holy mutiny?

REVOLUTION IS EXTREME

Years ago I sat right behind Lester Sumrall in a public meeting. By then Sumrall was at least eighty-two years old. His wife had already gone on to be with the Lord, and he himself had a great deal of difficulty seeing. During worship I watched as he held up this scrap of paper next to his eyes and began to write something on it.

For some reason I became curious. I wanted to know what he was writing down, which is totally unlike me. Just as I began to see it, he put the paper down. Then in a couple minutes, he lifted it up again and wrote something more on it. This time I was able to see what he had written. Sumrall wrote, "Lord, help me to love You more and to hate the devil more."

I have never forgotten that. Even at the age of eighty-two, Sumrall's passionate love for God led to a passionate hatred of the devil and a revolt against the devil and all his works.

Dutch Sheets, in his book *Authority in Prayer*, noted that phrases found in Ephesians 1, 2, 3, and 6 could be grouped together to form a powerful statement of our authority to operate in heavenly places and disrupt the authority of Satan.

Dutch omitted some of the "fillers" in the verses and formed one of those WOW declarations. Grasp and take in the compelling call to courage, strength, and anointing as you read what he put together:[3]

> Blessed be the God and Father of our Lord Jesus Christ, who has blessed us with every spiritual blessing in the heavenly places in Christ…which He brought about in Christ, when He raised Him from the dead, and seated Him at His right hand in the heavenly places…and raised us up with Him and seated us with Him in the heavenly places, in Christ Jesus…so that the manifold wisdom of God might now be made known through the church to the rulers and the authorities in the heavenly places….For our struggle is not against flesh and blood, but against the rulers, against the powers, against the world forces of this darkness, against the spiritual forces of wickedness in the heavenly places.
>
> —EPHESIANS 1:3, 20, 2:6, 3:10, 6:12, NAS

REVOLUTIONARY REPENTANCE

A call to revolution is a call to something extreme. It is a matter of life or death. In Christian terms, it is a call to live out the gospel with all of its radical claims. Above all, it is a call for the people of God to make an impact on their generation. It begins with the prophetic message of repentance.

Repentance is the essence of revolution. It is countercultural in and of itself. Repentance makes it possible for the people of God to regain the moral high ground that the enemy has captured and to thereby effect radical changes on the society around them.

Remember, repentance means to turn around. To turn around is to revolve, to experience a personal or corporate revolution.

JOIN THE REVOLUTION

If you believe, as most serious and committed Christians do, that we are in the midst of a revolution, words such as these will compel you to move forward:

> What happened to the days of old when men put their faces to the floor? They wanted to know God for themselves, but could they? In hopes to reach Him they would climb the highest mountain. Anything to be closer to where He may be. They wanted to talk to God. They wanted to pray for their families, their friends, their nations. They were desperate for revival, and wouldn't leave until they met with Him. They wanted to hear His voice for themselves. There was no futile distraction that could knock them off course.... Man's voice... could not stop them, or suppress their passion. Their heart was set. They would seek and find.... [4]

> The Revolution is a call to those who are listening. It requires sacrifice, commitment, and loyalty. It is neither for the coward nor the faint-hearted. It is for those willing to jump headfirst into the trenches and those willing to go to battle when others choose to run away. It is about bringing hope to the hopeless, truth to the lost, and freedom for those in captivity! It's about

giving oneself to a cause, and being willing to surrender a lifetime for a fight with the aim of making things better, when things might actually get worse.

The Revolution is about change. It is time for the church to rise out of our complacency and truly seek the God we claim to serve. It is time for the church to wake up and realize the war at hand. It is time for us to help the poor, help those in need, love those of differing opinions, rescue the perishing, and take a bold stand for truth when others are afraid!

Jesus was the ultimate revolutionary. He was a radical, and His words didn't always settle well with the "religious," yet He peacefully spoke with fearless authority. He knew who He was, and wasn't afraid of anything. At the same time He had an amazing compassion for people, and the love He exerted was revolutionary. He loved everyone, even the outcasts of society! He gave hope to the ones the "religious" condemned. He had a real passion for people, and gave us the ultimate example of what it means to truly love.

The Revolution is about uniting together and taking action to make an impact in history. It's about giving hope, truth, respect, and LOVE.

We hope to awaken you to realize the POWER OF ONE LIFE, YOURS. You can make a difference.[5]

Today there is a fire burning in the souls of many of Jesus's followers. It is not just the young who are zealous. This fire burns hot in the hearts of people of all ages.

I'll never forget the first time I saw Dutch Sheets speak in about the year 2000. It was in Dallas, Texas. I saw such a fire in his eyes, such an intensity in his face, and I heard such a seriousness in his voice that it almost seemed like anger. It was not anger; it was a holy indignation crying out over the prevailing condition of the United States of America. It was fierce. The revolutionary edge was clear.

Some people call the younger generation the "revolution generation" because young people are zealous and impatient by nature. Members of the younger generation chomp at the bit in their urgency to change the system as it currently exists. They see the hypocrisy; they feel the heartlessness; they want to expose the motives. They long for the realization of an idyllic, ultimate model of reality. They are intense, dead serious, and, at times, argumentative in their desperation to see change.

Jesus gravitated toward the young and impatient ones when He chose His disciples, who were men in their twenties. Jesus said, "Zeal for [My Father's] house has eaten Me up" (Ps. 69:9; John 2:17).

That same spirit seems to possess these young revolutionaries.

I asked a member of this generation, a young woman named Esohe Osai, to help me understand more about the battle over the affections of the eighteen- to twenty-five-year-olds in the United States today. Esohe is a world changer. She is a leader who works with inner-city Detroit teenagers, teaching them in a premier charter school.

Esohe earned her bachelor's degree from the University of Michigan and her master's degree from Harvard. She has a heart for the emerging generation and is passionate about effecting change. Here is what she wrote for me about her generation:

> A typical eighteen- to twenty-five-year-old in America is pulled in different directions by various lusts—lusts for instant gratification, material things, technology, superficial connections, prominence and celebrity status, and so forth. A cursory view of MTV or BET will reveal much about our generation and

the ways we give preference to superficial things: sex, but no intimacy or real bond; music with lyrics that convey nothing worthwhile or meaningful. Richard Foster, author of *Celebration of Discipline*, says, "Superficiality is the curse of our age."[6] Recently I read a report that stated that the majority of young adults consider their two most important life goals to be (1) getting rich, and (2) being famous.

Yet God's Word says He created our inmost beings in our mothers' wombs, and that we were created in God's image, which must mean that we are like Him, with many facets and much depth. The New Testament tells us that God's wisdom is imparted to us as the Spirit searches the deep things of God. We were not created to be as superficial as this generation wants to be.

We are a generation of split affections. Affection can be measured by what one spends the most time and attention on. An individual can only have true affection for something that he or she *knows* about. The enemy is fully aware of this, so he keeps our minds filled with images of fame, wealth, and beauty. When we sing songs about lip gloss and how to party like a rock star, we reveal where our affections lie. Just look at the Billboard Top 10 singles to see the superficiality of the things that Generation Next is pursuing. And yet, God wants our affection, and He wants us to know Him.

An interesting twist on the word *affection* is that it comes from a Latin root word that means "influence." Affection is influence. Within our generation there is an ongoing battle between the influence of superficial celebrity status and the Spirit of the living God who searches out the deep things of God. The apostle Paul wrote to the Colossians about setting their affection on things above and not on things of the earth. The only way this can happen is if we pay more attention to the things above. This is the battle that we are waging daily.

David said in Psalm 27:4, "One thing have I desired of the Lord, that will I seek: that I may dwell in the house of the Lord all the days of my life, to behold the beauty of the Lord, and to inquire in His temple." If the body of Christ in Generation Next would become a generation of *one thing,* then we could influence our peers and win the victory in the battle against the enemy over the affections of our generation. We need to narrow our affection and claim our generation. We need to become a people who will cry out, "O God, let us be a generation that seeks Your face!"

ONE THING, A HUMBLE HEART

Whether you are a young person or a not-so-young person, a humble, seeking heart is the one thing that attracts God. I learned about this the hard way.

When I was young, I was an atheist for a while; then I was an agnostic. Something inside me was desperately empty. Though outwardly I was successful and fulfilled, inwardly I was miserable. Two questions consumed me: What is the meaning of life? What is the worth of my life?

One night I simply said, "God, if You exist, I have some things I need to talk over with You." I didn't say those words with emotion. My words seemed cold, calculating, and flat. But as soon as the words were out of my mouth, Jesus walked into my room. I literally felt the door to my spirit and soul open up, and Jesus came in.

No one led me in a prayer of repentance. I didn't call a Christian television station and have someone pray with me. I simply said, in essence, "Help, God! I need You!"

Yet it wasn't the words that got God's attention. I had known for a long time that I was miserable. I was looking for answers. I had been reading constantly and had talked to anyone I thought might have answers.

But that night, I fell all the way down to humility. I humbled myself before God when I asked Him to help me understand. Then I stumbled on the truth of Scripture:

> On this one will I look: On him who is poor and of a contrite spirit, and who trembles at My word.
>
> —ISAIAH 66:2

God is always looking for *one thing* from me and from you, and that is a heart that is humble toward Him, a heart that is stripped of other gods and of other affections, a heart that is therefore pure in its desire. Before we can rise with Christ, we have to die with Christ. To die with Christ is to lose our own lives. I need to die to what I want, what I think, who likes me, who doesn't like me, what I look like, who my friends are, how big my business or my ministry is, how much money I have in the bank, how much education I have, what my status or position is, and on and on. All of us have, to some degree, at least one of these shameful elements in our lives.

Jesus Himself said that only when we, like a grain of wheat, fall into the ground and die, can we multiply. When we have given up our rights to do and to have, we gain true life. Then whatever we touch—that is in the will of God for us—will multiply exponentially in an awesome way that glorifies God. (See John 12:24–25.)

Paul said that your life and mine is hidden with Christ in God when we have died to ourselves (Col. 3:3). All the potential, the power, the creativity, the might, and the glory of God Himself are hidden in that new life. Therefore when I die to myself and come alive in Him, there is no limit to what I can produce because it's not about me or about my strength. It's all about God and His strength.

REVELATION LEADS TO TRANSFORMATION

To get to the level of change necessary to truly reform this nation, we need to realize that what it takes to change a society is the same thing that it takes to change an individual person. The scope of change is much greater in an entire society than it is in one person, but the process is the same.

It doesn't matter how phenomenal your ideas, visions, and dreams may be; you cannot effect true change, a holy revolution, until you have a pure and humble heart. By the same token, it doesn't matter how impressive the programs, solutions, and ideas of a society may be; they cannot make true progress until the mass of people who constitute that group or nation becomes desperate and realizes that they are at the end of themselves. Then transformation can occur. The revelation is that we need an awakening, individually as well as corporately. We just need God—desperately!

DESPERATE PRAYER BRINGS REVIVAL

Desperate crying out to God brings revival. Revival—which results in revolution within society—is not the product of people's efforts, but rather it is the product of God's response to their cries. Winkie Pratney, in his book *Revival: Principles to Change the World*, wrote that it is never the power of the preaching, but the presence of the Spirit of revival that creates dramatic results.[7]

159

Revival is more than just the return to life of God's people. True revivals result ultimately in the conversion of unbelievers and the transformation of society. This can be seen in the Welsh Revival, the Great Awakenings, the Hebrides Revival, and many more.

In the 1850s in Kalamazoo, Michigan, all the main Protestant churches gathered to unite in prayer. Someone stood up and read a woman's request that her husband be saved. A big, rough-looking guy stood up and said, "That must be me, because I have a praying wife and I know she prays for me. Will you pray for me now?" They prayed, and afterward the man sat down.

Then a cascade of men stood up, all saying the same thing. The Spirit of God fell in that place. More men began to sob under the convicting power of the Holy Spirit. In one night, four hundred men were saved.[8] You have to believe that many new believers had an impact on the society around them.

A similar thing happened in Louisville, Kentucky, in 1858, and the morals of the city were transformed positively. People said it was as if the Spirit of God were sitting on the city, brooding over it.[9] Transformed people create transformed societies.

STRATEGIC EVENTS AND TIMES

Some things change with one strategic event. Others unfold over time. Let me tell you an example of one strategic event that changed the course of history.

In 1993, Chuck Pierce and I were invited to speak at a citywide meeting with other Detroit leaders. The meeting was held in the very center of the city, in the Renaissance Center now owned by General Motors. About five hundred people were present.

As we were meeting, a high-profile court trial was taking place.

Malice Green was a black man who had been beaten to death by white police officers. The police officers were on trial, and the verdict was to be announced on the day of our last meeting. Already people had been bused in from all over the nation so they could riot in protest if, as expected, the verdict was supportive of the white police officers. It was a highly, racially charged face-off.

On the morning when I got up to speak, a spirit of repentance fell. I could not speak because people, being supernaturally led, started coming to the platform to repent. White people began to repent to black people, and vice versa. People began to repent of all sorts of things. God had walked into that meeting and hijacked it for His purposes. Neither Chuck nor I had ever seen anything like it, nor have we seen anything like it since.

For four hours, people wept and cried out for mercy, for deliverance, for forgiveness. All we could do is flow with what was happening. By the end of that meeting, all we knew was that God had come very sovereignly into that meeting in answer to the people's cries.

Then, to our amazement, the verdict came out. The police officers were judged to be guilty. A massive riot had been averted. The headline in *USA Today* the next morning said something like, "Riots Averted in Detroit."[10] Though *USA Today* knew nothing about the holy confrontation with racial hatred and injustice in that meeting room, we knew that God Himself had hijacked that meeting and, through our repentance, had turned a city around. Warriors had taken their places in humility before the holy God and had found there the place of victory.

Some things unfold over time. In January 2008, I visited Elk River, at the invitation of Rick Heeren. Rick works with Ed Silvosa as well as serving as the Global Apostolic Prayer Network leader for the state of Minnesota. He wanted me to personally see what was happening there.

Elk River is a town of around twenty-five thousand people. In 1995, pastors in that town began to gather to pray for their city, and something happened. God began to revolutionize their city. Pastors of different persuasions prayed together, including those from Lutheran, Alliance, charismatic, and Catholic churches. Their work of a united prayer—"God, we love our city; come and set up Your home in our midst!"—set in motion an invasion from heaven.

The pastors began to teach their people to go out into the world and make a difference. They taught them to establish the kingdom of God wherever they were assigned.

Business owners began to know God in a way they never had before. They captured the heart of God to release His heart and His kingdom in the marketplace. Businesses began to establish themselves on kingdom principles rather than worldly principles. Those businesses became not only places of commerce but also places where employees and customers could be ministered to.

Bible studies were started with employees who were interested. Prayer began to be held in the workplaces. Something began to change dramatically.

- A community Christian, kingdom-centered marketplace roundtable was established. Business owners and pastors started meeting monthly to pray and strategize together; their businesses were transformed. It has become a hotbed for innovative business ideas.

- One business in that community has now established more than six hundred churches in Ukraine and has placed the pastors on their payroll.

- A construction business started a ministry to help rebuild houses after Hurricane Katrina in Louisiana. That businessman had his best year economically in 2007, the worst year in recent history for the housing construction industry.[11]

- When the Harley-Davidson dealership came to town, the Christian businessmen went to welcome the dealer. Out of that contact the Harley-Davidson dealer became a Christian.

- Money is flowing into that city. Chuck Ripka is from that town, and he tells his story of starting a Christian bank in his book *God Out of the Box*.[12]

- Government has been affected. The mayor of that city is a committed Christian and also the longest serving mayor in the history of the town. More business is being attracted to that city. There is a miraculous unity among the pastors, business leaders, and mayor. I experienced this firsthand as I sat with them.

- The poor are being ministered to both spiritually and practically. The employees of the local Ford dealership held a garage sale and donated the money to the local food pantry. They have a heart for those in need.

- The education system is also being affected. You can read about it in *The Elk River Story* by Rick Heeren.[13] It is a modern-day story about what is happening.

Something is happening in Elk River. There is such a tangible presence of God in that town that people will exit off the I-94 freeway to come into the city. One person recently drove into the town, walked into one of the churches, an Alliance church, and asked the pastor to tell her what was happening in that city.

I too could feel the tangible presence of God when I was there. Furthermore, people are coming into a personal relationship with Jesus Christ because the leaders have decided to "undo, destroy, loosen, and dissolve the works the devil has done" in that city. (See 1 John 3:8.) The people are experiencing the leaders' hatred of the devil, their love for God, and resulting compassion for others.

City residents are now beginning to ask to know "their God." God's kingdom has come and His will is being done in Elk River, Minnesota.

KINGDOM TRANSFORMATION

I have led the Michigan State Global Apostolic Prayer Network since the mid-1990s. My leadership role means that I am a warrior who is called to take on the Goliath that is causing my state to decline or plateau as a righteous, just, and prosperous place. I am called and responsible—as are you—to initiate a process of transformation. My responsibility is to lead the state of Michigan into a position where the presence, power, and purpose of God are welcome in order to facilitate the transformation of the state.

Transformation is a process that is incremental in nature. Towns, cities, states, and nations are changed over time, not all at once. Scriptural injunctions are to be applied not only to individuals but also to cities, states, and whole nations:

> I appeal to you therefore, brethren *[or cities, states, nations]*, and beg of you in view of [all] the mercies of God, to make a decisive dedication of your bodies *[cities, states, nations]* [presenting all your members and faculties] as a living sacrifice, holy (devoted, consecrated) and well pleasing to God, which is your reasonable (rational, intelligent) service and spiritual worship. Do not be conformed to this world (this age), [fashioned after and adapted to its external, superficial customs], but be transformed (changed) by the [entire] renewal of your mind [by its new ideals and its new attitude], so that you may prove [for yourselves] what is the good and acceptable and perfect will of God, even the thing which is good and acceptable and perfect [in His sight for you].
>
> —ROMANS 12:1–2, AMP

When transformation occurs, a city, state, territory, or nation begins to be revolutionized for the good. Righteousness and justice are reestablished. The spiritual atmosphere makes God's presence available to the church—some call it an open heaven.

Government, the economy, education, and the church are affected positively. Society begins to flourish. Eventually the transformed city should become something like the Garden of Eden, a place where God dwells with His people and His people dwell with Him.

TRANSFORMATION IN PORT HURON

On June 15, 1962, Tom Hayden, a University of Michigan student, led a gathering in Port Huron, Michigan. Fifty-nine delegates from eleven campuses in our nation were looking for ways to change the culture of the United States of America.

The outcome of this gathering was the Port Huron Statement, which became the founding manifesto and handbook for the Students of a Democratic Society (SDS). On a national level, the SDS turned a younger generation away from God to humanism, free love, sexual immorality, drugs, and violence. It became the largest student-led, antiwar organization in the United States growing from six hundred members in 1963 to more than one hundred thousand in 1968. At its height, it organized the 1968 "10 Days of Resistance," the largest student strike in U.S. history.[14]

For the subsequent generation, Port Huron and its environs became demoralized. Families were destroyed through sexual immorality, alcohol, drugs, rebellion, and sexual abuse of children. Marriages constantly fell apart, and godly families were continually under attack with mental torment, overwhelming poverty, unexplained illnesses, out-of-wedlock pregnancies, accidents, and all kinds of abuse. One mayor of Port Huron was imprisoned for child sexual abuse. There was an alleged major connection from this area of Michigan to the Oklahoma City bombing of the Alfred P. Murrah Federal Building in 1995.[15] Anyone who visited this region would report they felt like they were under a cloud of oppression. It seemed as if the church and the Port Huron area were under a massive spiritual attack.

It also seemed that this event, the writing of the Port Huron Statement, had defiled the city and region that had granted access to its drafters. This action had laid the foundation for the defilement of not only the local territory but also for the United States, which went into an unremitting decline through lawlessness and the erosion of morals and character.

Both the Port Huron regional spiritual leaders and Cindy Williams, the Global Apostolic Prayer Network mobilizing coordinator for the state, were aware of the event that took place. However, they did not know how and when to address it.

Then in October 2006, James Nesbit of Prepare the Way Ministries, who is also a regional coordinator from the Illinois Global Apostolic Prayer Network, led a prayer initiative in the states surrounding the Great Lakes. The focus of this initiative was to neutralize the effect of demonic structures that had been brought into these states through the Great Lakes. Cindy worked with James in this endeavor where it concerned Michigan. A number of Michigan cities were included in this journey, including Port Huron.

When the team got to Lake Huron and started to pray over it, they experienced tremendous warfare. Port Huron is one of two key port cities on this lake, Detroit being the other. The state of Michigan is shaped like a giant mitten, and Port Huron is on the edge of the thumb. In fact, the region is known as the Thumb.

A team member had a vision that the water around the Thumb formed a serpent's mouth and the serpent's teeth were planted into the mid-part of the thumb, which would be Port Huron. It was seeking to kill the land and inhabitants of this area. The mouth of the enemy needed to be closed so the Thumb could be set free and could come into alignment with God's presence and purpose. How could the hand of Michigan operate properly if we did not restore the Thumb to full functioning?

Following this prayer initiative, Pastor Mark Seppo, the Global

Apostolic Prayer Network regional coordinator for the Thumb, initiated regular meetings with the pastors of the region, as well as with James and Cindy. They began to seek God about how to work together within the region and how to break through the spiritual resistance that was keeping the region from moving forward.

During one of these gatherings, a local pastor gave James and Cindy a copy of Robert Bork's book, *Slouching Toward Gomorrah*. This book historically reviews how the Port Huron Statement in 1962 became the most widely circulated anti-Christ document of that decade and brought SDS to national prominence, starting a national decline into ungodliness.

The pastors' conclusion following their review of the book was that they believed it was time to address and repent for the involvement of Port Huron in the Summer of Love. They could see that the church did not guard the "voice" that had been allowed to speak from their city. Consequently, Port Huron had become a gateway to a sweeping national rebellion, the "hippie revolution," which had led the next generation in a wrong direction, affecting the entire nation and from which we are yet to recover.

James Nesbit, Cindy Williams, Pastor Mark Seppo, and the pastors of the region wrote a repentance statement concerning the Port Huron Statement. Furthermore, they wrote a new decree addressing the issues described above. On the forty-fifth anniversary of the original event (June 15), two hundred pastors and intercessors gathered at the state park, the same site where the original document was conceived and written in 1962. They repented and issued the new decree, thus removing the reproach of the past sins and positioning Port Huron in right relationship with God. Because this is the Thumb, it would affect the entire hand, the state of Michigan.

Cindy reported that during the two-hour event, an unusual seed began to blow through the air. It looked as if it were snowing in the middle of June. It seemed that the seed represents a new planting, the spiritual harvest that would now be on the way, a sign that God was now free to plant anew and release a new harvest.

Powerful things began to happen. A month later, Chuck Pierce and I visited this region for a worship gathering. The gathering was unprecedented; the school auditorium was packed out. This city and region, which had been shut down spiritually, erupted in worship. They had never experienced such an open heaven. Chuck was not aware of the seed that had been blown in the wind a month before when he told the pastors prophetically, numerous times during this packed out gathering, that they were to prepare for the harvest, because God was bringing it in. We could hardly get through the meeting because spontaneous worship just kept erupting up and out of the people.

Here is what had happened: The presence of God had been reestablished in this territory through the genuine repentance of its spiritual leaders. Now God was welcome in this territory and transformation could begin to occur. His government had been reestablished.

Other significant things began to take place following this event. The city leaders announced the building of a new industrial plant, which would significantly increase the number of jobs in the region. Governmental shifts took place in the November 2007 elections. Two of the cities, Port Huron and Marine City, elected Christian mayors. The majority of their city councils' seats were filled with godly Christian leaders. Marine City's high school football team even won the state championship that year. It seemed that a powerful dark presence had been broken through and now God's government could come into place.

Through united prayer, the agreement of leaders, strategic repentance, the breaking of demonic strongholds, and the releasing of a new decree a whole region had moved into an entirely new place.

Goliath had been brought down. He had been "killed," and his head (rulership) had been chopped off!

Now the territory is positioned to continue toward complete transformation. God's presence is tangibly present in this area of Michigan, and positive expectation has returned to the people.

FACING OFF WITH GOLIATH, WINNING TRUE REVIVAL

What is your part in this unfolding battle? As you seek the Lord with all your heart, He will begin to give you a heart for specific people and situations.

I always ask myself, "What makes me cry?" What makes me cry is what God is preparing me to heal. Second, I ask myself, "What makes me mad?" When something makes me mad, God is grooming me to right that wrong. I also need to grow in knowing Him, living in His presence, and tapping into His resources. Where He is, there will be victory. So I watch for His presence. You will become strong in the Lord through your union with Him, drawing your strength from His boundless strength. You need to:

> Put on God's whole armor [the armor of a heavy-armed soldier which God supplies], that you may be able successfully to stand up against [all] the strategies and the deceits of the devil. For we are not wrestling with flesh and blood [contending only with physical opponents], but against the despotisms, against the powers, against [the master spirits who are] the world rulers of this present darkness, against the spirit forces of wickedness

in the heavenly (supernatural) sphere. Therefore put on God's complete armor, that you may be able to resist and stand your ground on the evil day [of danger], and, having done all [the crisis demands], to stand [firmly in your place].

—EPHESIANS 6:11–13, AMP

Before, during, and after you win your way to victory against the enemy, you need to keep standing strong. You need to be ready when your Goliath shows up. Goliath is alive and well today, and he is taunting you right now.

Different "Davids" hear different taunts from different Goliaths. I am reminded of Davids like Jane Hansen Hoyt, who has led Aglow International to take on three major Goliath initiatives—male-female reconciliation, standing with Israel, and unraveling the threat of Islam. I also think of Dutch Sheets, who has heard the Goliath taunt over the United States that has echoed through the halls of the Supreme Court. Then there's the many unknown prayer teams who travel to unknown places of this nation and the world, doing God's bidding and changing neighborhoods, cities, states, and nations. There are the leaders who, out of the heart of God for the disenfranchised, are going into the darkest places of cities to preach the gospel to the poor, including practical help on how to become equipped to do a job that will reverse their poverty. There are those leaders hearing the heart cry of the orphans and the widows who are reaching out with compassion to lift up the hands that hang down and strengthen their feeble knees. They are warriors, going in to loose the bands of wickedness holding people in darkness.

Yes, Goliaths are taunting us wherever we live and worship. In the state in which I live, Michigan, twin Goliaths of unemployment and housing foreclosures are causing people to leave the state in droves. Anywhere in the nation, what about the Goliath of abortion? Racism? The state of the church itself? Don't forget the two kinds of Islamic Goliaths—the one that is radical and fanatical and that plans the demise of the West, as well as the one that is *not* radical and fanatical, but that is nevertheless wearing a veil of deception because it has been empowered by the prince of Persia.

As you can see, there is no shortage of opposition. There is only a shortage of resolve and strength on the part of the people of God. What about you? Have you taken your place in the battlefield? Has your name been listed in the roll call of the army of God? Are you stepping up in the strength that God supplies, as David did when he stepped out before Goliath, having declined to wear the armor of human crafting so that he could step forward humbly reliant on God and armed only with what he needed for decisive victory?

Put on your personal suit of heavenly armor and hear the call once more. Here is the passage from Ephesians that I quoted just above, this time from The Message paraphrase:

> And that about wraps it up. God is strong, and he wants you strong. So take everything the Master has set out for you, well-made weapons of the best materials. And put them to use so you will be able to stand up to everything the Devil throws your way. This is no afternoon athletic contest that we'll walk away from and forget about in a couple of hours. This is for keeps, a life-or-death fight to the finish against the Devil and all his angels.
>
> Be prepared. You're up against far more than you can handle on your own. Take all the help you can get, every weapon God has issued, so that when it's all over but the shouting you'll still be on your feet. Truth, righteousness, peace, faith, and salvation are more than words. Learn how to apply them. You'll need them throughout your life. God's Word is an indispensable weapon. In the same way, prayer is essential in this ongoing warfare. Pray

hard and long. Pray for your brothers and sisters. Keep your eyes
open. Keep each other's spirits up so that no one falls behind or
drops out.

—EPHESIANS 6:10–18, THE MESSAGE

You and I are being invited to become warriors, a generation of
warriors who will join the revolution. God is inviting us to love Him
more and hate the devil more, as He did Lester Sumrall. He is inviting
us to join Him in righteous indignation, to receive a violent spirit that
is empowered by God. He is calling us to engage our heart, to take up
our weapons, to walk with Him, and to war with Him. In every aspect
of this present war, we are not to be frightened or overcome, because we
do not go forth in our own power to fight Goliaths; we go in the name
of the Lord.

Paul had a word for the church at Philippi that is fitting for us today
as we leave to go out to battle. We have a great privilege before us—to
have faith in Christ as well as to suffer with Him. We too are to wage
war as Paul did. "This honour have all his saints" (Ps. 149:9, KJV)!

And do not [for a moment] be frightened or intimidated in
anything by your opponents and adversaries, for such [constancy
and fearlessness] will be a clear sign (proof and seal) to them of
[their impending] destruction, but [a sure token and evidence]
of your deliverance and salvation, and that from God. For you
have been granted [the privilege] for Christ's sake not only to
believe in (adhere to, rely on, and trust in) Him, but also to
suffer in His behalf. So you are engaged in the same conflict
which you saw me [wage] and which you now hear to be mine
[still].

—PHILIPPIANS 1:28–30, AMP

10

The Kingdom Has Come— Awaken the Revolutionaries

T HE LONGER I SPOKE, THE STRONGER THE VISION came. I was in Jakarta, Indonesia, in July of 2007, and I was preaching at three services back to back, beginning Saturday evening. While I was focused on speaking to the people who were present and sitting there in the congregation, something strange was happening. It was as if I was someplace far away. I seemed to have tuned into something far beyond this gathering. The audience was attentive, hanging on to every word. Even as I spoke, I found myself wondering, questioning.

I kept seeing this supernatural picture, which the Bible calls a vision, superimposed on what I was viewing with my physical eyes— the people sitting there. Where was I? What was I seeing? What did it mean? How should I respond? How did it affect the people? Did it affect them at all?

Here I was, preaching on the fact that God was doing a "new thing." I felt almost embarrassed because I had expounded on this topic so many times before. A few years earlier, there had been a season when I had not been able to preach anything else, so now I felt it was almost blasphemous to approach that subject. I had preached on it so often and for so long in the past that now I felt as if I were beating a dead horse...except

I couldn't not preach it again this time. I couldn't get away from this driving message in my heart: *God is doing something new.*

This time at least the scriptural focus was not Isaiah 43:18–21, as it had been in the past. It was Isaiah 42:9: "Behold, the former things have come to pass, and new things I now declare; before they spring forth I tell you of them" (AMP). That aspect of the current situation was a wee bit comforting, although not much.

What in the world was God saying? Why could I not get away from this message? It was frustrating, particularly because the message was so indefinable, intangible, veiled. Furthermore, the more I preached it, the stronger the vision became that stood between the people and me. Here was this "other world" picture superimposing itself on top of the crowd in front of me, an overlay of a vision. It was worse than having a fly continuously landing on my nose and diverting my attention.

THE MOUNTAIN OF THE KINGDOM

What was the vision? As I preached, I saw this mountain that was beginning to arise out of the waters of the sea. Just the tip of the mountain was out of the water. I knew that the rest of the mountain was there, still submerged, but it was no longer hidden from my awareness. It was in the process of being unveiled. I was captivated by this picture. As I progressed through my message, I also pondered the vision's meaning. Some scriptures came to mind. (Scripture should interpret any vision that we experience.)

I realized that the mountain was speaking of a kingdom, the kingdom of God. In the Book of Daniel, I remembered that the mountain or kingdom had started with one stone, one person, one leader. It went on to become the one that overcame every other kingdom:

You, O king, were watching; and behold, a great image! This great image, whose splendor was excellent, stood before you; and its form was awesome. This image's head was of fine gold, its chest and arms of silver, its belly and thighs of bronze, its legs of iron, its feet partly of iron and partly of clay. You watched while a stone was cut out without hands, which struck the image on its feet of iron and clay, and broke them in pieces. Then the iron, the clay, the bronze, the silver, and the gold were crushed together, and became like chaff from the summer threshing floors; the wind carried them away so that no trace of them was found. And the stone that struck the image became a great mountain and filled the whole earth....

And in the days of these kings the God of heaven will set up a kingdom which shall never be destroyed; and the kingdom shall not be left to other people; it shall break in pieces and consume all these kingdoms, and it shall stand forever. Inasmuch as you saw that the stone was cut out of the mountain without hands, and that it broke in pieces the iron, the bronze, the clay, the silver, and the gold—the great God has made known to the king what will come to pass after this. The dream is certain, and its interpretation is sure.

—DANIEL 2:31–35, 44–45

This mountain that represents the kingdom of God was set into motion with that one stone, Jesus Christ. (I mentioned it earlier in chapter 5 when I was talking about the stone that David used to kill Goliath.) As each member, each living stone, is added to Christ's kingdom, the mountain (the kingdom) grows. The greater the revelation individuals possess of Jesus Christ and His kingdom, the greater the power of the kingdom.

Seas often represent people. In the vision, the mountain was beginning to arise out of the sea in a visible way. Just the tip was observable, yet I knew the rest of the mountain, the kingdom yet to be uncovered, was there. In other words, the people, represented by the sea, are beginning to experience and release a revelation not just of Jesus Christ but also of His rulership as King of kings and Lord of lords, the King of the kingdom of God. They know who He is and what He rules. They know that He has birthed a kingdom that will overtake in time every other kingdom. That means we, the people of the remnant church, are in the time of the revelation of the kingdom of God as not just a spiritual reality but as a reality that will visibly transform the world.

BRINGING KINGDOM RULE

In early 2008, I attended the National Charismatic Summit, where David Shibley and I participated on the same panel, "Is the Charismatic Movement Making a Difference?" He got right to the heart of the issue. This is what he said:

- Moves of God are not the end game. The kingdom of God is.

- The process for bringing kingdom rule is through evangelism and discipleship, i.e., the Great Commission.

- Revivals do two things: birth movements and transform people.

- Revival-birthed movements transform society. (Revivals bring us into the presence of God so that we can hear the directive *rhema* word of God, both personally and corporately. Obedience to this *rhema* is what brings changes in our society.)

This means that we are in the day when the church is arising and releasing the kingdom of God. As we carry out our first and primary mandate, to evangelize and disciple new believers, the kingdom will grow both numerically and authoritatively. These disciples, people like you and me, will be transformed. Movements will arise and spread throughout the earth in a wave of transformation that will revolutionize society. How will this happen? Not through great ideas coming from men's minds. This rolling-out of the kingdom of God and this rolling-over of every other power will happen as you and I listen to what God is saying to us, to His *rhema*, and then do what He tells us to do and say what He tells us to say.

Our actions will begin to change us, not only personally but also in our families, neighborhoods, churches, cities, states, and nations. True leaders will arise who do not use their newfound positions for self-aggrandizement but who will begin to release the anointing without arrogance, power without pride, and boldness without brashness.[1]

This means that you and I are on the forefront of the emergence of the last great move of God, the releasing of His kingdom in the earth today. This kingdom begins through our capturing God's heart for people as well as the nations who do not know Him. It begins with the Great Commission. Then we continue to listen to God and obey Him, and we begin to release the kingdom of God everywhere we go. Our actions, big or small, significant or seemingly insignificant, are all part of the rolling-out of the kingdom.

Everything the kingdom of God touches becomes transformed. Jesus said in Luke 11:20 that if He by the finger of God cast out devils, then the kingdom of God had come to that person. That is the thesis of Daniel 2: God's kingdom overtakes every other kingdom.

Jesus came as the King of kings and Lord of lords. He overcame every power and principality. He came to disrupt the powers that be. He came to unseat thrones and kingdoms. He didn't come with a secret agenda; He announced it to all. His agenda was not a destructive one. Instead, He brought back to life those who had died, released into freedom those who were bound, and restored sight to those who were blind. He healed the crippled so they could run, skip, and leap like calves let out of a stall. Now you and I are no longer blind. Because the kingdom of God has come to us, we can envision what can happen through Jesus Christ.

Jesus came as a revolutionary. He started a revolution when He came and gave away His life. He furthered it when He sent His Holy Spirit to empower each one of His followers. Yes, Jesus was a revolutionary, and His revolt was over Satan and his kingdom. He came to unseat the devil and all his works. This is what Jesus said about Himself:

> The Spirit of the LORD is upon Me,
> Because He has anointed Me
> To preach the gospel to the poor;
> He has sent Me to heal the brokenhearted,
> To proclaim liberty to the captives
> And recovery of sight to the blind,
> To set at liberty those who are oppressed;
> To proclaim the acceptable year of the LORD.
>
> —LUKE 4:18–19

Warriors, awaken your revolutionary nature and passion! You have been invited to perceive this kingdom vision and to come into this kingdom mandate. The mountain of the kingdom of God is beginning to be seen. It is on the move. It is arising out of God's church and moving through His people. This kingdom will overcome every other kingdom, bringing passionate love for God, compassionate love for people, and absolute and utter hatred of the devil and his works.

This kingdom will grow and gradually overcome every other kingdom:

> Now it shall come to pass in the latter days
> That the mountain of the LORD's house
> Shall be established on the top of the mountains,
> And shall be exalted above the hills;
> And peoples shall flow to it.
> Many nations shall come and say,
> "Come, and let us go up to the mountain of the LORD,
> To the house of the God of Jacob;
> He will teach us His ways,
> And we shall walk in His paths."
> For out of Zion the law shall go forth,
> And the word of the LORD from Jerusalem.
> He shall judge between many peoples,
> And rebuke strong nations afar off;
> They shall beat their swords into plowshares,
> And their spears into pruning hooks;
> Nation shall not lift up sword against nation,
> Neither shall they learn war anymore.
> But everyone shall sit under his vine and under his fig tree,
> And no one shall make them afraid;

For the mouth of the LORD of hosts has spoken.
For all people walk each in the name of his god,
But we will walk in the name of the LORD our God
Forever and ever.
"In that day," says the LORD,
"I will assemble the lame,
I will gather the outcast
And those whom I have afflicted;
I will make the lame a remnant,
And the outcast a strong nation;
So the LORD will reign over them in Mount Zion
From now on, even forever.
And you, O tower of the flock,
The stronghold of the daughter of Zion,
To you shall it come,
Even the former dominion shall come,
The kingdom of the daughter of Jerusalem."
— MICAH 4:1–8, EMPHASIS ADDED

You and I—as members of the church of Jesus Christ, the King of kings and Lord of lords—are about to experience the former dominion, *the kingdom of the daughter of Jerusalem.* The kingdom of God is both at hand (as close to us as our own hand) and within us. We are not meant to lead an ordinary life. We have been created to be warriors, revolutionaries who release the kingdom of God on earth.

Do you see it? The mountain of the Lord, the kingdom of God, is arising out of the sea of God's people to turn the world upside down *and* right side up. We're ordinary people, you and I. And yet we have been invited to step up. As we refuse to be intimidated by the circumstances of our world but rather are astounded with the greatness of

Christ and His kingdom, He shall bring His rule into the midst of chaos and disaster. We are revolutionaries, love-constrained warriors who, like Jesus, so love the world that we give up our rights to what we want, and we give ourselves away to God and His purposes. In losing our lives we will find true life. Simple people, simple faith, powerful results, giant-killers!

Warriors, awaken! Launch the revolution! Arise and stand to your feet. Go forth and release the kingdom everywhere you go!

11

A Final Word

IT WAS 5:40 A.M. I STRUGGLED TO WAKE up. I had just finished dreaming something that I believed was significant, and I was trying to remember it—because I knew it was to be included in this book. It was to be a final word that would provide perspective to our outlook on this war. As I fought my way back to consciousness, I began to remember what I had dreamed...the dream rehearsed a vision I had experienced.

THE VISION

In April of 2006, I was speaking at a conference. During the worship service, an unusual presence of God began to settle upon me. The heavier God's presence came, the more caught up I became, caught up in a heavenly realm. I found myself in the middle of an IMAX or 3-D-like experience; it was as if I were in the middle of this action movie.

I saw this unusually large number of people coming toward me. As I looked to see who they were, I noticed that they were all men. Furthermore, all of them were dressed like rugged ancient men, scruffy-looking, strong and muscular, almost scary, wearing animal skins. They had swords and clublike weapons, axes, bows and arrows, and shields. Many of them were on horses. The best way to describe that army is to liken them to the army in the movie *Braveheart*. I began to realize that they formed a massive army.

All of them were running toward their enemy, rushing toward me in an attack mode. I asked the Lord, "Are they for us or against us?"

He said to me, "They are for you."

As soon as the Lord answered me, it was as if I were taken up into the sky to the altitude where the jets fly. I looked down on the United States. As I looked down, I saw that there were very few lights on anywhere in the nation. It looked like very rural or remote places I had flown over where there was one light here and another light there, far removed from each other. However, as this army galloped across the nation, lights began to turn on in the places that the army was moving through. Furthermore, the lights remained on in the places they had already moved through. The lights grew until cities and towns were like massive lit-up places across the nation.

Going back to Earth, I saw that the army galloping across this nation was not deterred by anything. This army galloped through walls, buildings, obstructions, fences—anything that stood in its way. Nothing slowed them down or stopped them. They were supernatural in strength and courage. There was no hesitation in them. It was as if someone had placed a computer chip inside of them that said, "Straight ahead; don't stop or look back until you have reached the other side of the nation." Billboards, buildings, houses flew every which way as they galloped right through them.

The further they advanced, the more lit-up the nation was, until there were huge areas where the lights had become contiguous. What had been dark now became fully lit. I looked down on fully lit, almost blindingly bright cities, towns, and even rural areas.

The Lord said, "This is My army." I was cognizant that as we (you and I) joined with the Lord, rising up as a warrior generation, God would loose His army. It is a heavenly army, the host of heaven, which will fight with and for us. He, the Lord of Hosts, will go before us. He will lead them and us, and together we will break through every resistant place.

I thought of the word picture that the prophet Micah painted. I'm quoting it here in two translations, so that you can see it better in your mind's eye:

> The Breaker [the Messiah] will go up before them. They will break through, pass in through the gate and go out through it, and their King will pass on before them, the Lord at their head.
>
> —MICAH 2:13, AMP

> I will surely gather all of you, O Jacob;
>> I will surely bring together the remnant of Israel.
> I will bring them together like sheep in a pen,
>> like a flock in its pasture;
>> the place will throng with people.
> One who breaks open the way will go up before them;
>> they will break through the gate and go out.
> Their king will pass through before them,
>> the LORD at their head.
>
> —MICAH 2:12–13, NIV

I knew I had seen a breakthrough army, because nothing could stop them. Once the army was commissioned to action, they were neither deterred nor slowed; they kept moving across this nation until all of the lights were on. I knew I had seen a picture of how this army would fight until a massive awakening occurs across this nation, a revival as well as an awakening; a revival of life, righteousness, healing, deliverance, salvation, utter abandonment to God, fervent passion, and an awakening of the those who have not known God to His reality, His authenticity, His validity.

Joel describes an army that is similar to this army. The difference is that the army Joel describes is one of judgment. The army I saw was going before us to break through every hindrance and obstacle for the purpose of restoring God's kingdom on Earth. However, for purposes of description, Joel expresses best what the army that I saw in the vision looks like.

Blow the trumpet in Zion;
>   sound the alarm on my holy hill.
Let all who live in the land tremble,
>   for the day of the LORD is coming.
It is close at hand—
>   a day of darkness and gloom,
>   a day of clouds and blackness.
Like dawn spreading across the mountains
>   a large and mighty army comes,
such as never was of old
>   nor ever will be in ages to come.
Before them fire devours,
>   behind them a flame blazes.
Before them the land is like the garden of Eden,
>   behind them, a desert waste—
>   nothing escapes them.
They have the appearance of horses;
>   they gallop along like cavalry.

With a noise like that of chariots
    they leap over the mountaintops,
like a crackling fire consuming stubble,
    like a mighty army drawn up for battle.
At the sight of them, nations are in anguish;
    every face turns pale.
They charge like warriors;
    they scale walls like soldiers.
They all march in line,
    not swerving from their course.
They do not jostle each other;
    each marches straight ahead.
They plunge through defenses
    without breaking ranks.
They rush upon the city;
    they run along the wall.
They climb into the houses;
    like thieves they enter through the windows.
Before them the earth shakes,
    the sky trembles,
the sun and moon are darkened,
    and the stars no longer shine.
The LORD thunders
    at the head of his army;
his forces are beyond number,
    and mighty are those who obey his command.

               —JOEL 2:1–11, NIV

We are not to be frightened in this battle. The Lord will go before us and fight for us. All we have to do is follow Him and obey Him. The battle belongs to the Lord.

Something is about to happen in this nation. The Captain of the Hosts is about to commission His army into action. You and I, the warrior generation, will join with Him. A holy revolution is about to begin!

> Lift up your heads, O you gates!
> And be lifted up, you everlasting doors!
> And the King of glory shall come in.
> Who is this King of glory?
> The LORD strong and mighty,
> The LORD mighty in battle.
> Lift up your heads, O you gates!
> Lift up, you everlasting doors!
> And the King of glory shall come in.
> Who is this King of glory?
> The LORD of hosts,
> He is the King of glory.
>
> —PSALM 24:7–10

Notes

Chapter 1
A Rude Awakening

1. J. R. R. Tolkien, *The Lord of the Rings* (Boston: Houghton-Mifflin, 1993), 698.

Chapter 2
Waking Up With Goliath

1. Barbara J. Yoder, *The Breaker Anointing* (Ventura, CA: Regal, 2004), 48.

2. Biblesoft's New Exhaustive Strong's Numbers and Concordance with Expanded Greek-Hebrew Dictionary. Copyright © 1994, Biblesoft and International Bible Translators, Inc., s.v. OT:6428, *"palash,"* OT:6429, *"Peleseth,"* and OT:6430, *"Pelishtiy."*

3. Judith Voigt, *Alexander and the Terrible, Horrible, No Good, Very Bad Day* (New York: Aladdin, 1972), 1.

4. E-mail to author relating prophetic word given by Barbara Wentroble and Keith Pierce at Glory of Zion Church, Sunday, August 12, 2007. Original transcript available at http://www.glory-of-zion.org/outmail/8-13-07_EcuadorTripReportOnline.htm (accessed August 21, 2008).

Chapter 3
Goliath Stands Before Us

1. Eamonn Kelly, *Powerful Times* (Upper Saddle River, NJ: Wharton School Publishing, 2006).

2. Alan Nelson, "Church on the Horizon," *Rev!* magazine, September/October 2006, 65–66.

3. For parts of this evaluation, I am indebted to Bobby Brewer, who identified the issues of relativism, absence of Christian beliefs, pluralism, and spiritual curiosity in the Nelson article cited above.

4. From a presentation by Ron Luce in January of 2007 at Strang Communications in Lake Mary, Florida.

5. Andrew Maykuth, "Philadelphia Leads Big Cities in Murder Rate," *Philadelphia Inquirer*, June 5, 2007, http://www.philly.com/inquirer/home_top_stories/20070605_Phila__leads_big_cities_in_murder_rate.html (accessed August 18, 2008).

6. Fox Butterfield, "Guns Used More for Suicide Than for Homicide," *New York Times*, October 17, 1999, at http://query.nytimes.com/gst/fullpage.html?res=9C05E5D81F30F934A25753C1A96F958260 (accessed August 18, 2008).

7. "Teen Suicide: Statistics, Signs, and Facts," Family First Aid: Help for Troubled Teens, http://www.familyfirstaid.org/suicide.html (accessed August 18, 2008).

8. "Teen Suicide Rate: Highest Increase in 15 Years," *Science Daily*, September 8, 2007, http://www.sciencedaily.com/releases/2007/09/070907221530.htm (accessed August 18, 2008).

9. "Suicide Trends Among Youths and Young Adults Aged 10–24 Years—United States, 1990–2004," *Morbidity and Mortality Weekly Report* 56, no. 35 (September 7, 2007): 905–908; http://www.cdc.gov/MMWR/preview/mmwrhtml/mm5635a2.htm (accessed August 18, 2008).

10. Citymayors.com, "Tacoma Named as the Most Stressful U.S. City," January 10, 2004, http://www.citymayors.com/features/us_stresscities.html (accessed August 18, 2008).

11. Suicide.org, Suicide Statistics, http://www.suicide.org/suicide-statistics.html (accessed August 18, 2008).

12. Joel C. Rosenberg, *Epicenter: Why Current Rumblings in the Middle East Will Change Your Future* (Carol Stream, IL: Tyndale House, 2006).

13. Lionel Tiger and Robin Fox, *The Imperial Animal* (New York: Holt, Rinehart and Winston, 1971).

14. Edie Weiner and Arnold Brown, *FutureThink* (Upper Saddle River, NJ: Pearson Prentice Hall, 2006), 130.

15. Ibid., 130–131.

16. Kelly, *Powerful Times*, 134. See also Samuel P. Huntington, *The Clash of Civilizations and the Remaking of World Order* (New York: Simon & Schuster, 1998).

17. Weiner and Brown, *FutureThink*, 145.

18. Ibid., 132.

19. Ibid.

20. Philip Yancey, *Reaching for the Invisible God: What Can We Expect to Find?* (Grand Rapids, MI: Zondervan, 2000), 90–91.

CHAPTER 4
GOLIATH DEMANDS A DAVID

1. From *Preaching and Preachers,* Martyn Lloyd-Jones, 117, as quoted in Colin C. Whitaker, *Great Revivals* (Springfield, MO: Radiant Books, 1984), 15.

2. Whitaker, *Great Revivals,* 15.

3. Reclaim7Mountains.com, "Transcript of Interview of Loren Cunningham on Original 7 Mountains Vision," November 19, 2007, http://www .reclaim7mountains.com/apps/articles/default.asp?articleid=40087& columnid=4347 (accessed August 18, 2008).

4. Philip Yancey, *Soul Survivor: How Thirteen Unlikely Mentors Helped My Faith Survive the Church* (New York: Galilee, a division of Doubleday, 2003).

5. Biblesoft's New Exhaustive Strong's Numbers and Concordance with Expanded Greek-Hebrew Dictionary. Copyright © 1994, Biblesoft and International Bible Translators, Inc., s.v. OT:1732, "David" and OT:1730, "*dowd.*"

CHAPTER 6
A VIOLENT SPIRIT

1. Karlyn Bowman, "The Passionless Public: Why Americans Are Tuning Out," American Enterprise Institute for Public Policy Research, June 1, 2001, http://www.aei.org/publications/pubID.12883/pub_detail.asp (accessed August 19, 2008).

2. Erwin Raphael MacManus, *An Unstoppable Force: Daring to Become the Church God Had in Mind* (Orange, CA: Yates and Yates LLP, 2001), 8.

3. From *The Awakening* by Friedrich Zuendel, as related in Steve Fry, "The Martyr's Heart," *Kairos,* July/August 2007, 39–40.

CHAPTER 7
FAITH THAT SPEAKS, CREATES

1. Jessie Penn-Lewis, *The Centrality of the Cross* (Fort Washington, PA: Christian Literature Crusade, n.d.), 32.

2. Gary Fields and John Ritter, "In Detroit, Muted Anger, Relief; Determined City Avoids Violence," *USA Today*, August 24, 1993, 03.A.

3. Dutch Sheets, *Authority in Prayer* (Minneapolis MN: Bethany House, 2006), 91.

CHAPTER 8
THE HEART OF THE BATTLE

1. Author's recollection, reiteration, and account of points gleaned from the book *Waking the Dead* by John Eldredge (Nashville: Thomas Nelson, 2003).

2. Mother Teresa, *Come Be My Light,* ed. Brian Kolodiejchuk (New York: Doubleday, 2007).

CHAPTER 9
THE TIME FOR REVOLUTION

1. Winkie Pratney, *Revival: Principles to Change the World* (Springdale, PA: Whitaker House, 1983), 322–327.

2. Whitaker, *Great Revivals*, 25.

3. Sheets, *Authority in Prayer*, 111.

4. JointheRevolution.org, "Manifesto," http://www.jointherevolution.org/html/about.htm (accessed August 20, 2008).

5. JointheRevolution.org, "The Revolution: What Is It?" http://www.jointherevolution.org/html/index.htm (accessed August 20, 2008).

6. Richard J. Foster, *Celebration of Discipline: The Path to Spiritual Growth* (New York: HarperCollins, 1988), 1.

7. Pratney, *Revival: Principles to Change the World*.

8. Ibid., 82.

9. J. Edwin Orr, *The Fervent Prayer: The Worldwide Impact of the Great Awakening of 1858* (Chicago, IL: Moody Press, 1974), 22.

10. Fields and Ritter, "In Detroit, Muted Anger, Relief; Determined City Avoids Violence."

11. Robert Schroeder, "U.S. Housing Starts, Permits Fall To 12-Year Low," The MarketWatch, September 19, 2007, http://www.marketwatch.com/news/story/us-housing-starts-permits-fall/story.aspx?guid=%7B3EC37A64-D471-4937-9631-096ACFCF9CE3%7D (accessed September 8, 2008).

12. Chuck Ripka with James Lund, *God Out of the Box* (Lake Mary, FL: Charisma House, 2007).

13. Rick Heeren, *The Elk River Story: Transforming the Spiritual Climate of a City* (San Jose, CA: Transformational Publications, 2004).

14. Facts were obtained from the following sources: Vanessa Huang, "Radical Politics," *The Boston Phoenix*, February 9, 2006, http://thephoenix.com//Boston/News/3739-Radical-politics/ (accessed August 20, 2008). Mark Rudd, "The Death of the SDS," *The Student Underground*, May 20, 2005, http://markrudd.com/Homepage/Death%20of%20SDS.htm (accessed August 20, 2008). Giuseppe Lojacono, "The Sixties in the United States," translated from the Italian and published as part of the World *Conflicts Documents Project*, http://www.geocities.com/iturks/html/the_sixties_in_usa1.html (accessed August 20, 2008).

15. Constitutional Rights Foundation, "The Aftermath of Terror," *Bill of Rights in Action*, Fall 1995, updated July 2000, http://www.crf-usa.org/bria/bria11_4.html (accessed August 20, 2008).

CHAPTER 10
THE KINGDOM HAS COME—AWAKEN THE REVOLUTIONARIES

1. These thoughts were inspired by the comments of David Shibley in the panel discussion, "Is the Charismatic Movement Making a Difference?" at the National Charismatic Summit, hosted by Stephen Strang in January 2008.

OTHER BOOKS BY BARBARA J. YODER

The Breaker Anointing
God's Bold Call to Women
The Overcomer's Anointing (August 2009)

For more information about Shekinah Christian Church, Breakthrough Leadership Institute, and/or Breakthrough Apostolic Ministries (Network), as well as other resources available from Barbara J. Yoder, please write or call:

Shekinah Christian Church

P. O. Box 2485

Ann Arbor, Michigan 48106

Telephone: (734) 662-6040

Fax: (734) 662-5470

E-mail: pastorbarbara@shekinahchurch.org

http://www.shekinahchurch.org

FREE NEWSLETTERS
TO HELP EMPOWER YOUR LIFE

Why subscribe today?

☐ **DELIVERED DIRECTLY TO YOU.** All you have to do is open your inbox and read.

☐ **EXCLUSIVE CONTENT.** We cover the news overlooked by the mainstream press.

☐ **STAY CURRENT.** Find the latest court rulings, revivals, and cultural trends.

☐ **UPDATE OTHERS.** Easy to forward to friends and family with the click of your mouse.

CHOOSE THE E-NEWSLETTER THAT INTERESTS YOU MOST:

- Christian news
- Daily devotionals
- Spiritual empowerment
- And much, much more

SIGN UP AT: **http://freenewsletters.charismamag.com**

8178